Marie McLisky

English for
BANKING
in Higher Education Studies

Course Book

Series editor: Terry Phillips

English for Specific Academic Purposes

Garnet
EDUCATION

Published by
Garnet Publishing Ltd.
8 Southern Court
South Street
Reading RG1 4QS, UK

First published 2008
Reprinted 2008

ISBN 978 1 85964 935 0

British Cataloguing-in-Publication Data
A catalogue record for this book is available from
the British Library.

Production
Series editor: Terry Phillips
Project management: Louise Elkins, Martin Moore
Editorial team: Jane Gregory, Rebecca Snelling
Academic review: Sheila Scott
Design: Henry Design Associates and Mike Hinks
Photography: Sally Henry and Trevor Cook; Alamy (Lou
Linwei, Ramer Unkel), Corbis (Jose Fuste Raga, TOPhoto),
Fotosearch, Shutterstock, Clipart.com, Digital Vision,
Stockbyte
container ship on page 55: © Adrian Shafto, Johnson
Stevens Agencies; OECD image on page 71: © OECD.

Audio recorded at Motivation Sound Studios produced by
EFS Television Production Ltd

The author and publisher would like to thank Google for
permission to reproduce the results listings on page 35.
Every effort has been made to trace copyright holders and
we apologize in advance for any unintentional omission. We
will be happy to insert the appropriate acknowledgements
in any subsequent editions.

Printed and bound in Lebanon by International Press

Introduction

English for Banking is designed for students who plan to take a banking course entirely or partly in English. The principal aim of *English for Banking* is to teach students to cope with input texts, i.e., listening and reading, in the discipline. However, students will be expected to produce output texts in speech and writing throughout the course.

The syllabus focuses on key vocabulary for the discipline and on words and phrases commonly used in academic and technical English. It covers key facts and concepts from the discipline, thereby giving students a flying start for when they meet the same points again in their faculty work. It also focuses on the skills that will enable students to get the most out of lectures and written texts. Finally, it presents the skills required to take part in seminars and tutorials and to produce essay assignments.

English for Banking comprises:

- student Course Book
- the Teacher's Book, which provides detailed guidance on each lesson, full answer keys, audio transcripts and extra photocopiable resources
- audio CDs with lecture and seminar excerpts

English for Banking has 12 units, each of which is based on a different aspect of banking. Odd-numbered units are based on listening (lecture/seminar extracts). Even-numbered units are based on reading.

Each unit is divided into four lessons:

Lesson 1: vocabulary for the discipline; vocabulary skills such as word-building, use of affixes, use of synonyms for paraphrasing

Lesson 2: reading or listening text and skills development

Lesson 3: reading or listening skills extension. In addition, in later reading units, students are introduced to a writing assignment which is further developed in Lesson 4; in later listening units, students are introduced to a spoken language point (e.g., making an oral presentation at a seminar) which is further developed in Lesson 4

Lesson 4: a parallel listening or reading text to that presented in Lesson 2 which students have to use their new skills (Lesson 3) to decode; in addition, written or spoken work is further practised

The last two pages of each unit, *Vocabulary bank* and *Skills bank*, are a useful summary of the unit content.

Each unit provides between 4 and 6 hours of classroom activity with the possibility of a further 2-4 hours on the suggested extra activities. The course will be suitable, therefore, as the core component of a faculty-specific pre-sessional or foundation course of between 50 and 80 hours.

It is assumed that prior to using this book students will already have completed a general EAP (English for Academic Purposes) course such as *Skills in English* (Garnet Publishing, up to the end at least of Level 3), and will have achieved an IELTS level of at least 5.

For a list of other titles in this series, see www.garneteducation.com/

Book map

Vocabulary focus	Skills focus		Unit
• words from general English with a special meaning in banking • prefixes and suffixes	Listening	• preparing for a lecture • predicting lecture content from the introduction • understanding lecture organization • choosing an appropriate form of notes • making lecture notes	**1**
	Speaking	• speaking from notes	
• English–English dictionaries: · headwords · definitions · parts of speech · phonemes · stress markers · countable/uncountable · transitive/intransitive	Reading	• using research questions to focus on relevant information in a text • using topic sentences to get an overview of the text	**2**
	Writing	• writing topic sentences • summarizing a text	
• stress patterns in multi-syllable words • prefixes	Listening	• preparing for a lecture • predicting lecture content • making lecture notes • using different information sources	**3**
	Speaking	• reporting research findings • formulating questions	
• computer jargon • abbreviations and acronyms • discourse and stance markers • verb and noun suffixes	Reading	• identifying topic development within a paragraph • using the Internet effectively • evaluating Internet search results	**4**
	Writing	• reporting research findings	
• word sets: synonyms, antonyms, etc. • the language of trends • common lecture language	Listening	• understanding 'signpost language' in lectures • using symbols and abbreviations in note-taking	**5**
	Speaking	• making effective contributions to a seminar	
• synonyms, replacement subjects, etc. for sentence-level paraphrasing	Reading	• locating key information in complex sentences	**6**
	Writing	• writing complex sentences • reporting findings from other sources: paraphrasing	
• compound nouns • fixed phrases from banking • fixed phrases from academic English • common lecture language	Listening	• understanding speaker emphasis	**7**
	Speaking	• asking for clarification • responding to queries and requests for clarification	
• synonyms • nouns from verbs • definitions • common 'direction' verbs in essay titles (*discuss, analyse, evaluate*, etc.)	Reading	• clauses with passives	**8**
	Writing	• paraphrasing • expanding notes into complex sentences • recognizing different essay types/structures: · descriptive ·analytical · comparison/evaluation · argument • writing essay plans • writing essays	
• fixed phrases from banking • fixed phrases from academic English	Listening	• using the Cornell note-taking system • recognizing digressions in lectures	**9**
	Speaking	• making effective contributions to a seminar • referring to other people's ideas in a seminar	
• 'neutral' and 'marked' words • fixed phrases from banking • fixed phrases from academic English	Reading	• recognizing the writer's stance and level of confidence or tentativeness • inferring implicit ideas	**10**
	Writing	• writing situation–problem–solution–evaluation essays • using direct quotations • compiling a bibliography/reference list	
• words/phrases used to link ideas (*moreover, as a result*, etc.) • stress patterns in noun phrases and compounds • fixed phrases from academic English • words/phrases related to online security	Listening	• recognizing the speaker's stance • writing up notes in full	**11**
	Speaking	• building an argument in a seminar • agreeing/disagreeing	
• verbs used to introduce ideas from other sources (*X contends/accepts/asserts that* ...) • linking words/phrases conveying contrast (*whereas*), result (*consequently*), reasons (*due to*), etc. • words for quantities (*a significant minority*)	Reading	• understanding how ideas in a text are linked	**12**
	Writing	• deciding whether to use direct quotation or paraphrase • incorporating quotations • writing research reports • writing effective introductions/conclusions	

1 WHAT IS BANKING?

A Read the text. The red words have familiar meanings in general English. What is the meaning of each word in banking?

> It was the last day of the holiday. Tomorrow, the new term started. Their boat was floating under the branch of a large tree.
> 'We'll have to return soon,' said May.
> 'I know, I know,' replied Adam, 'I'll open the engine compartment and fix it.'
> 'Why don't you call them?'
> 'If they have to come out, we'll lose our deposit.'
> 'We'll miss our train at this rate,' said May.

B Read the conversation below. Complete each sentence with one of the red words from Exercise A. Change the form if necessary (e.g., change a noun into a verb).

A: Good afternoon. I'd like to _____ an investment account.

B: Do you want the account at this _____ ?

A: Yes, please.

B: Right. How much do you want to _____ ?

A: £20,000. What's the best _____ I can get?

B: It depends on the _____ . Do you want your money on _____ or on a _____ term?

A: Well, I'm not sure. What's the highest _____ I can earn?

B: Currently, the highest is a 6% fixed for two years, as opposed to the _____ rate on call. You'll find it's a good rate compared with other banks.

A: OK. I'll take it.

C Study the words in box a.

1 What is the connection between all the words?
2 What is the base word in each case?
3 What do we call the extra letters?
4 What is the meaning of each prefix?
5 Can you think of another word with each prefix?

> **a**
> decentralized dishonour
> illegal illegible inactive
> insufficient international
> invalid irregular miscalculate
> recall transaction

D Study the words in box b.

1 What is the connection between all the words?
2 What is the base word in each case?
3 What do we call the extra letters?
4 What effect do the extra letters have on the base word?
5 Can you think of another word with each suffix?

> **b**
> bancassurer circulation
> commercial convertible creditor
> debtor depreciation investment
> liability liquidity monetary
> negotiable payable regulatory
> security speculative variable

E Discuss the illustrations on the opposite page using words from this page.

1

3-year
SAVINGS BOND
5.5%

STAR SAVINGS BANK

2

Euro-US dollar

(line graph showing Euro-US dollar exchange rate from July to March, ranging between 1.14 and 1.30, with x-axis labels July, Sept, Nov, Jan, March)

3a

ANW Bank
Water Street Branch
Water Street
Barton BT4 6NP

'50-30-99

Date 1... ... 2006

Pay _____ Antonia Marcos _____

_____ Two hundred pounds only _____

Account payee

£ (200:00)

P R Lee

PRLee

000009••50-30-99:•005486389••95

3b

Available balance:
£149.63

4

STATEMENT

ANW Bank
Current account

	IN	OUT	BALANCE
FROM PREVIOUS STATEMENT			650.55
MAXWELL ST		5.99	644.56
9037 04921 CHB	159.20		803.76
E-STORE 2665		15.24	788.52
DIRECT DEBIT		8.00	780.52
FUND TRANSFER		102.49	678.03

A You are a student in the Banking Faculty of Hadford University.

   1 Write a definition of banking.

   2 What other ideas will be in this lecture? Make some notes.

   See *Skills bank*

B 🎧 Listen to Part 1 of the talk. Which heading below best describes this part of the talk? Tick the best choice.

   a Money-lending services   _____

   b The history of banking   _____

   c The origins of English words in banking   _____

   d Buildings where banking services are provided   _____

Credit Suisse Group headquarters, Zürich, Switzerland

C In Part 2 of the talk, the lecturer defines a bank.

   1 Which do you think is the best definition?

      a It is not a financial institution.   _____

      b It is a government authority.   _____

      c It is a service organization.   _____

      d It is a government-licensed organization.   _____

   2 🎧 Listen and tick the definition chosen by the lecturer.

Alliance & Leicester, UK

D In Part 3 of the talk, the lecturer describes different types of bank.

   1 How many types of bank can you think of?

   2 What sort of person or organization does each type of bank work with?

   3 🎧 Listen, make notes, and check your ideas.

E 🎧 In the final part of the talk, the lecturer gives a definition of banking and some examples. Listen and mark each word in the box **D** if it is part of a definition and **E** if it is part of an example.

> banking services _____   financial instruments _____
> national legislation _____   mortgages _____
> pension funds _____   share certificates _____
> time deposits _____

F Write a definition of banking. Use more than one sentence if necessary. Use words from Exercise E.

G Look back at your notes from Exercise A. Did you predict:

   • the main ideas?

   • most of the special vocabulary?

The European Central Bank

1.3 Extending skills

lecture organization • choosing the right kind of notes

A What can you ...

1 deposit?   3 negotiate?   5 recall?

2 fix?   4 transfer?   6 issue?

B How can you organize information in a lecture? Match the beginnings and endings.

1 question and

2 problem and

3 classification and

4 advantages and

5 comparison and

6 cause and

7 sequence of

8 stages of a

9 theories or opinions then

contrast

definition

disadvantages

effect

events

supporting information

process

solution

answer

C How can you record information during a lecture?
Match the illustrations with the words and phrases in the box.

tree diagram   flowchart   headings and notes   spidergram   table   timeline   two columns

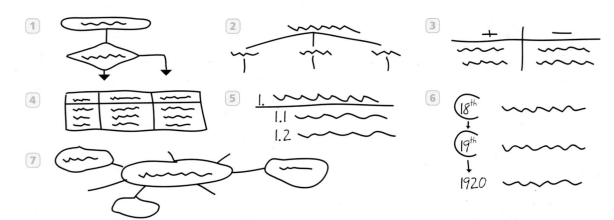

D Match each organization of information in Exercise B with a method of note-taking from Exercise C. You can use one method for different types of organization.

E 🎧 Listen to some lecture introductions. Choose a possible way to take notes from Exercise C in each case.

Example:

You hear: *Today we're going to look at key developments in establishing a global monetary standard over the last 200 years or so.*

You choose: *timeline*

A   Read these captions and match them to the pictures.

    a   From an ATM, clients can access their accounts at any time, on any day of the week.

    b   The gold standard defined a national currency in terms of a fixed weight in gold.

    c   Electronic machines are used to verify money, that is, check it for counterfeit notes.

    d   The US dollar, euro, pound sterling and Japanese yen are all hard currencies.

    e   Commercial banks today provide their clients with mortgage finance and loans for other consumer goods.

B   🎧 Cover the opposite page. Listen to the lecture introductions from Lesson 3 again. Make an outline on a separate sheet of paper for each introduction.

C   Look at your outline for each lecture. What do you expect the lecturer to talk about in the lecture? In what order?

D   🎧 Listen to the next part of each lecture. Complete your notes.

E   Uncover the opposite page. Check your notes with the model notes. Are yours the same or different?

F   Work in pairs.

    1   Use the notes on the opposite page. Reconstruct one lecture.

    2   Give the lecture to another pair.

① Effects of MNBs/foreign banks

+	–
lower costs (for MNB)	competition for domestic banks (↓ profitability)
can increase efficiency of domestic banks	financial guarantees in event of bank failure?

② Organizational structure of banks

	centralized	decentralized
authority	kept at top level	some delegated to lower levels
accountability	top level	some can be delegated
decision-making	not as quick in larger organizations; more effective in stable environment; more coordination; greater influence of leadership from top	quicker than large centralized organizations; more effective in uncertain environment

③ Why are banks regulated?

1 Economic role of banks
Banks must not fail ∴ regulatory controls
(e.g., exchange controls)

2 Need to protect customers
Regulations help protect customers from bank collapse

3 Prevention of banking collapse
Central bank as 'lender of last resort'; FDIC

4 Competition
Legislative restrictions (e.g., branching restrictions – though don't apply to bank holding companies)

5 Scope of banking activities
Restrictions imposed by many countries (e.g., banks not allowed to engage in non-financial activities; restrictions on services they can provide) ⟶ provide stability in banking system

④ Global monetary regime/standard

(= fixed exch. rate for currency)

early C19	Britain gold std. for pound, gold coins
↓	
mid C19	Germany gold std. then Scand., France, Jap.
↓	
1900	US gold std.
↓	
1930s	gold std. abandoned most countries (depression)
↓	
after WW1	£ = key currency
↓	
after WW2	$ = key currency
↓	
today	currencies pegged to hard currencies (e.g., $, €, £, ¥ or 'basket' of currencies

⑤ Modern technology + banking

Processing cheques

bank teller enters cheque details onto system → computer reads magnetic code → money debited from payer's a/c electronically → cheque sent to clearing house → money credited to payee's a/c

EFT (electronic funds transfer)

customer presents EFTPOS card → EFTPOS card debits customer's a/c → retailer's a/c credited → accounts updated/transactions processed overnight

ATMs (automated teller machines)

customer inserts ATM card → machine asks for PIN number → machine asks which transaction customer wants → if withdrawal, customer keys in amount → machine returns card + pays money

Guessing words in context

Using related words

Sometimes a word in general English has a special meaning in banking.

Examples:
ceiling, cap, branch

If you recognize a word but don't understand it in context, think:
What is the basic meaning of the word? Does that help me understand the special meaning?

Example:
*The **ceiling** is the highest part of a room. So the **ceiling** for bank interest rates must mean the highest rate.*

Removing prefixes

A **prefix** = letters at the **start of a word**.
A prefix changes the meaning of a word.

Examples:
resell – sell again
invalid – not valid

If you don't recognize a word, think: *Is there a prefix?* Remove it.
Do you recognize the word now? What does that prefix mean?
Add it to the meaning of the word.

Removing suffixes

A **suffix** = letters at the **end of a word**.
A suffix sometimes changes the **part of speech** of the word.

Examples:
transact + ion = verb ➜ noun
regulat + ory = verb ➜ adjective

A suffix sometimes changes the meaning **in a predictable way**.

Examples:
invest + or – a person who does something
secur + ity – noun expressing a condition

If you don't recognize a word, think: *Is there a suffix?* Remove it.
Do you recognize the word now? What does that suffix mean?
Add it to the meaning of the word.

Making the most of lectures

Before a lecture ...

Plan
- Find out the lecture topic.
- Research the topic.
- Check the pronunciation of names and key words in English.

Prepare
- Get to the lecture room early.
- Sit where you can see and hear well.
- Bring any equipment you may need.

During a lecture ...

Predict
- Listen carefully to the introduction. Think: *What kind of lecture is this?*
- Write an outline. Leave space for notes.
- Think of possible answers/solutions/effects, etc., while the lecturer is speaking.

Produce
- Write notes.
- Record sources – books/websites/names.
- At the end, ask the lecturer/other students for missing information.

Making perfect lecture notes

Choose the best way to record information from a lecture.

advantages and disadvantages	➜ two-column table
cause and effect	➜ spidergram
classification and definition	➜ tree diagram/spidergram
comparison and contrast	➜ table
facts and figures	➜ table
sequence of events	➜ timeline
stages of a process	➜ flowchart
question and answer	➜ headings and notes

Speaking from notes

Sometimes you have to give a short talk in a seminar on research you have done.
- Prepare the listeners with an introduction.
- Match the introduction to the type of information/notes.

2 THE ORIGINS OF BANKING

| 2.1 Vocabulary | using an English–English dictionary |

A How can an English–English dictionary help you understand and produce spoken and written English?

B Study the dictionary extract on the opposite page.

1 Why are the two words (top left and top right) important?
2 How many parts of speech does the word *bankrupt* have?
3 What do the superscript numbers mean after the word *bank*?
4 What do the numbers 1–4 mean in the definitions for the word *bank*?
5 Say the word *account*. Where is the stress?
6 Where is the stress in *bank account*?
7 What is the pronunciation of *a* in each bold word in this extract?
8 What is the pronunciation of *c* in each bold word in this extract?
9 What part of speech is *bankable*?
10 Are both of these correct? *He is a bankrupt/He is bankrupt.*
11 Can we say *I banked today*. Why (not)?

C Look at the bold words in the dictionary extract on the opposite page.

1 What order are they in?
2 Write all the words in the blue box in the same order.

D Look at the top of this double page from an English–English dictionary.

1 Which word from the blue box will appear on this page?
2 Think of words before and after some of the words in the blue box.

reduce   request

E Look up the red words in a dictionary.

1 How many meanings can you find for each word?
2 What kind of noun/verb is each one?
3 Which meaning is most likely in a text about banking?

charter   vault   deposit   note
mint   credit   money   regulate
financial   giro   receipt
negotiable   reserve   withdraw

F Look up the green words.

1 Where is the stress in each word?
2 What is the sound of the underlined letter(s) in each word?
3 Which meaning is most likely in a text on banking?

G Test each other on the words from Exercises E and F. Give the dictionary definition of one of the words. Can your partner guess which word you are defining?

H Discuss the illustrations on the opposite page using words from this lesson.

band

bankrupt

band /bænd/ *n* [C] a range of numbers with set upper and lower limits within which the movement of something, e.g., the rate of exchange, is restricted

bank¹ /bæŋk/ *n* [C] 1. a registered financial institution which receives deposits from its clients, provides credit and generally trades in money 2. the building used by such a business 3. *v* [T] the act of depositing money in a bank: *The company banks the takings every day.* 4. *v* [I] ~*with* to have an account with a bank: *I bank with ANW bank.*

bank² /bæŋk/ *n* [C] the side of a river

bankable /'bæŋkəbl/ *adj* acceptable to a bank as security for a loan

bank account /'bæŋk əˌkaʊnt/ *n* [C] an arrangement between a bank and a customer allowing the customer to make monetary transactions through the bank

bank advance /'bæŋk ədˌvaːns/ *n* [C] same as **bank loan**

bank balance /'bæŋk ˌbæləns/ *n* [C] the monetary position of a customer's bank account at a specific point in time

bank base rate /bæŋk 'beɪs reɪt/ *n* [C] also known as **repo rate**; acts as a benchmark rate for setting all other interest rates

bank bill /'bæŋk bɪl/ *n* [C] 1. BrE a bill of exchange issued by one bank telling another bank (usually in another country) to pay money to the holder by a due date 2. BrE same as **banker's bill** 3. AmE same as **banknote**

bank card /'bæŋk kaːd/ *n* [C] a card issued by a bank that automatically withdraws funds from the customer's account

bank charges /'bæŋk ˌtʃaːdʒɪz/ *pl n* charges made by a bank for carrying out customer services (AmE **service charge**)

bank charter /'bæŋk ˌtʃaːtə(r)/ *n* [C] an official government document incorporating a bank and specifying its rights

bank cheque /'bæŋk tʃek/ *n* [C] a cheque issued on a bank on behalf of the customer

bank credit /'bæŋk ˌkredɪt/ *n* [U/C] a borrowing facility, such as an overdraft, available to a customer from a bank

bank deposits /'bæŋk dɪˌpɒzɪt/ *pl n* money deposited in banks by their customers

bank draft /'bæŋk draːft/ *n* [C] a document issued by one bank ordering the payment of money to someone by another bank

banker /'bæŋkə(r)/ *n* [C] a senior executive of a bank

banker's draft /'bæŋkə(r)z ˌdraːft/ *n* [C] a draft drawn on a bank against the customer's own account or cash deposit

bankrupt /'bæŋkrʌpt/ *n* [C] 1. a person who cannot pay their debts 2. *adj* unable to pay one's debts

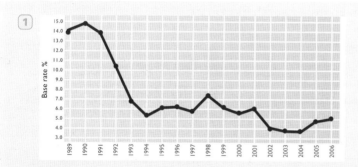

A What was the first significant innovation in the history of banking? If you don't know, guess!

B Study the table of contents on the right.

   1 What does each item mean? If you don't know, guess.
   2 How did it improve banking at the time?
   3 Are any of these innovations relevant today?

C You are going to read a text. What should you do before you read a text in detail?

D This text is about early banking services in Europe.

   1 Think of some research questions before you read.
   2 Compare your questions with those in the Hadford University assignment on this page.
   3 Look quickly through the text and write down all the dates.
   4 What is the best way to record this information?

E Study these sentences from the text and answer the questions below.

The first safe-deposit vaults were operated by royal palaces and temples.

The Greeks developed money in the form of silver and bronze coins.

During the Middle Ages, European monarchs controlled the production, or minting, of coins.

By the 17th century, goldsmiths were issuing additional receipts against the gold to borrowers.

The 1882 Bills of Exchange Act defined banking as trading in money by investing, lending or exchanging it.

   1 What are the banking services mentioned in this text?
   2 Where do you expect to find the answer to each question in the Hadford University assignment? Write 1, 2 or 3 next to the sentence.

F Read the text on the opposite page and check your ideas.

See *Skills bank*

Contents

HADFORD *University*

Faculty: Banking
Assignment 4

Do some research into early banking services in Europe.

Make notes to answer these questions.

1 When did the service develop?
2 Who developed the new service?
3 What prompted the new service?
4 Why was this service important?

BANKING from the Egyptians to the Victorians

The first safe-deposit vaults were operated in ancient Egypt by royal palaces and temples. Receipts were issued to those who deposited their goods in these vaults and written orders were required for withdrawals from them. The common form of money at that time was precious metals in weighed quantities. However, the written withdrawal orders became a more convenient method of payment.

In Alexandria, in the Ptolemaic period (305–30 BCE), granaries were organized into a network of state grain banks. Their main accounts were recorded in a central bank. This bank network operated as a giro system. Payments were transferred from one account to another without the physical exchange of money.

The ancient Greeks developed money in the form of silver and bronze coins around 600 BCE. Counting coins was much quicker and more convenient than weighing them, so the use of coins for everyday transactions spread rapidly. Greek bankers developed other services, including money-changing services, because of the variety of coins used. They developed a credit system which provided merchants with finance to pay for the shipping of their goods.

During the Middle Ages, European monarchs controlled the production, or minting, of coins. The value of the royal coins often exceeded their metallic value and minting costs. The English monarchs recalled all the coins and issued new ones every few years. This enabled them to reduce the circulation of counterfeit coins and make a profit from the metals used.

In the 13th century, Italy rose as a leader in commerce and industry. The Italian merchants helped revive commercial (merchant) banking. During the 14th century, the Bardi and Peruzzi families ran the major banking houses. Their banks collapsed, however, due to large and imprudent loans to the kings of England and Naples. The result was a financial panic, which had a serious effect on the economy. The Medici family established their own banks in the 15th century. These banks had connections to Germany as well as to financial centres in northern Europe. Banking in continental Europe was controlled by wealthy private bankers and powerful statesmen for more than 300 years.

In England in 1571, Sir Thomas Gresham built the first Royal Exchange. He obtained large loans from financiers in Antwerp. He was also banker to a series of monarchs from Henry VIII to Elizabeth I. But it was the London goldsmiths who laid the foundations for British banking. They issued deposit receipts, verifying ownership, to customers who deposited gold and silver with them. At first, the receipts simply proved that a certain amount of silver or gold had been deposited, but later the use of the receipts extended beyond that of reclaiming deposits. They became a form of exchange between traders in settling transactions. They were a convenient alternative to handling coins or precious metals, and so operated as paper money. This practice eventually led to the use of banknotes in England.

By the 17th century, goldsmiths were issuing additional receipts against the gold to borrowers. This meant the receipts on the gold exceeded the value of the gold reserves held. The result was an increase in the money supply. This system only worked so long as the original depositors did not withdraw all their deposits at the same time. There are other goldsmith banking functions that are relevant today. They include the development of demand and time deposits, balance sheets and promissory notes. In 1704 the English courts passed The Promissory Notes Act. The negotiable nature of the promissory note meant that the bearer or person holding the note was entitled to payment on it.

The 1882 Bills of Exchange Act defined banking as trading in money by investing, lending or exchanging it. This Act defined a bill of exchange as a note drawn on a banker and payable on demand. These demand notes are the precursors of the cheques we use today.

2.3 Extending skills
topic sentences • summarizing

A Study the words in box a. They are all used as nouns in the text you read in Lesson 2.

> **a** bank system gold giro
> money notes receipts
> deposit reserves supply

1 Give the common meanings of each word.

2 Put the words into pairs that have a meaning in banking.

B Study the words in box b.

> **b**   withdrawal payment
> transaction metallic imprudent
> reclaim depositor negotiable

1 What is the base word in each case? What part of speech is the base word?

2 Does the prefix/suffix change the part of speech?

3 How does the prefix/suffix change the meaning of the base word?

C Look back at the topic sentences from the text in Lesson 2. What information comes after each topic sentence? Suggest possible content.

Example:

> The Greeks developed money in the form of silver and bronze coins.

Why coins were developed (quick to count and convenient); how they were used (everyday transactions)

D Write a summary of the text on page 17. Paraphrase the topic sentences. Add extra information and examples. **See Skills bank**

2.4 Extending skills
using research questions • writing topic sentences • summarizing

A Can you remember all the early European banking innovations from Lesson 2?

B The lecturer has asked you to research *early American banking*.

1 Think of good research questions before you read the text.

2 Look quickly at the text on the opposite page. What is the best way to record information in this case while you are reading?

C Study the text on the opposite page.

1 Highlight the topic sentences.

2 Read each topic sentence. What will you find in the rest of the paragraph?

3 Which paragraph(s) will probably answer each research question? Read those paragraphs and make notes.

4 Have you got all the information you need? If not, read other paragraphs.

D Use the Internet to research one of the early banking services from the list in Lesson 2. Use the same research questions as in Lesson 2.

1 Make notes.

2 Write a series of topic sentences which summarize your findings.

3 Report back to the other students. Read out each topic sentence then add extra details.

The History of American Banks

The First Bank of
the United States

THE BANK OF NORTH AMERICA, established in 1781, was the first bank chartered by the United States government. Although it was privately owned, it operated as the government's bank and issued paper banknotes. These were promises to pay the bearer on demand. Banks had to maintain adequate reserves of gold to meet demands for repayment of the notes. Individual North American states chartered other large banks to issue banknotes. These banks focused on making short-term loans. Many were forced into bankruptcy. This was because they had over-extended their lending.

The First Bank of the United States was chartered by the federal government in 1791. It was established to serve both the government and the public. It ran into conflict with the state-chartered banks. They objected to the domination of the popular First Bank of the United States notes, which were seen to be safer than other banknotes. The government failed to renew its charter and the bank ceased trading in 1811. A second Bank of the United States was chartered in 1816. It ceased trading in 1836, due to opposition from local bankers and lack of federal government support. The years from 1837 to 1863 are referred to as the 'Free Banking Era'. In this era, American banking was represented by state-chartered banks. There was no federal regulation, and no consistency in the laws controlling the operation of the banks. This lack of regulation resulted in bank fraud, and many banks failed.

In the early 1800s, New York State created a fund to which each member bank contributed. The fund operated like a fractional reserve system, as this was money that the banks could not lend out. It was held as security for the banknote holders, in the event that the bank failed. New York became the world's financial centre after the completion of the Erie Canal in 1825. Its local banks had provided the capital for the construction of the canal.

The American Civil War (1861–1865) resulted in a change in the monetary system and new legislation. The war needed funding. The need to use metals for war meant coins were scarce. The 1863 National Bank Act led to the establishment of the Office of the Comptroller of the Currency. This office had the power to issue national bank charters. This created a dual banking system. Banks could operate under either a national or federal charter. The act also led to the production of national banknotes as a unified national currency. Only banks operating under the national charter were allowed to issue a national banknote. All national banknotes were backed by US government bonds, or US Treasury securities. National banks were required to keep a significant volume of bonds on deposit with the Comptroller of the Currency. In exchange, the banks received banknotes worth 90 per cent of the value of the bond held.

The state banks encouraged their customers to open demand deposit accounts. Withdrawals from these accounts were made by writing a cheque. Cheques, as a substitute for paper or coin currency, became well established. Between 1873 and 1907 they outnumbered banknote circulation. Some banks experienced liquidity problems. At times, the banks did not have enough cash, or liquid assets that could be changed quickly into cash. These banks could not honour their depositors' cheques and went out of business.

In 1907, a large number of depositors in New York City attempted to withdraw their money at the same time. The result was the Wall Street Panic. This spread across the United States as banks suspended withdrawals. Thirty-one national banks and 212 state banks collapsed. In response, the 1913 Federal Reserve Act was passed to re-establish a central bank, the Federal Reserve Bank. The act divided the nation into 12 districts. It established a regional Federal Reserve Bank in each district. To regulate and control the banks, the act set up the Federal Reserve System. Membership for national banks is compulsory. For state banks, however, membership is optional.

Using your English–English dictionary

This kind of dictionary helps you actually learn English.

Using headwords and parts of speech

1 Find the correct **headword**.
   These **bold** words in a dictionary are in alphabetical order. Look at the words on the top left and top right of the double page. Find a word which comes just before and after your word.

2 Find the correct **meaning**.
   If there are different meanings of the word, they appear in a numbered list. Look at all the meanings before you choose the correct one in context.

3 Find the correct **part of speech**.
   Sometimes the same headword appears more than once, followed by a small number. This means the word has more than one part of speech, e.g., *n* and *v*. Work out the part of speech before you look up a word.
   Clues:
   • Nouns come after articles (*a/an/the*) or adjectives.
   • Verbs come after nouns or pronouns.

Learning to pronounce words

The symbols after the headword show you how to pronounce the word. Learn these symbols (the key is usually at the front or the back of the dictionary).

The little line in the symbols shows you how to stress the word.

Example:
'*authorize* /ˈɔːθəraɪz/ but *au'thority* /ɔːˈθɒrətɪ/

Learning to use words correctly in context

Nouns can be **countable** or **uncountable**. This information is important for using articles and verb forms (e.g., *is/are*) correctly. Look for the symbol [**C**] or [**U**].

Some verbs need an object. They are **transitive**. Some verbs don't need an object. They are **intransitive**. This information is important for making good sentences. Look for the symbol [**T**] or [**I**].

Some words can be spelt in **British** English (e.g., *colour*, *centre*) or **American** English (e.g., *color*, *center*). Choose the correct spelling for the text you are working on.

Doing reading research

Before you start reading ...

- Think of research questions. In other words, ask yourself: *What must I find out from my research?*
- Look at headings, sub-headings, illustrations. Look for patterns or variations in presentation, e.g., a series of dates; words in **bold** or *italic* script. Think: *What information do they give me?*
- Decide how to record information from your reading. Choose one or more methods of note-taking. **See Unit 1** *Skills bank*

While you are reading ...

- Highlight the topic sentences.
- Think: *Which paragraph(s) will probably give me the answer to my research questions?*
- Read these paragraph(s) first.
- Make notes.

After reading ...

- Think: *Did the text answer all my research questions?*
- If the answer is no, look at other paragraphs to see if the information is there.

Using topic sentences to summarize

The topic sentences of a text normally make a good basis for a summary. Follow this procedure:

- Locate the topic sentences.
- Paraphrase them – in other words, rewrite them in your own words so that the meaning is the same. Do not simply copy them. (This is a form of plagiarism.)
- Add supporting information – once again, in your own words.

Example:

Paraphrase of topic sentence	*The first safe-deposit system was created in the vaults of royal palaces and temples.*
Supporting information and examples (summarized)	*They issued receipts to the depositors. Written orders were needed to withdraw goods.*

- Check your summary. Check that the ideas flow logically. Check spelling and grammar. If your summary is short, it may be just one paragraph. Divide a longer summary into paragraphs.

3 BANKING INSTITUTIONS

A Discuss these questions.

1 What services do banks commonly provide?

2 How many different types of banks can you name?

3 Look at your answers to questions 1 and 2. Where does the main stress fall

   a in each word?   **b** in each phrase?

> **a**
>
> credit cards   foreign investments
> insurance   mortgage finance
> online banking   personal banking
> personal loans   securities
> share capital   telephone banking
> text message banking   trade services

B Study the pictures on the opposite page.

1 What banking services are shown?

2 Match the pictures with words from box a.

C Complete each sentence with words from box a. Change the form if necessary.

1 The term _____ refers to both investments in stocks and shares, and the ownership certificates.

2 The bank accepted the bill of exchange from the exporter's overseas customer as part of its _____ for its client.

3 The value of a company's assets held as shares is known as _____ .

4 If you have a cell phone, _____ is so convenient.

5 At the first sign of trouble in the domestic economy he moved his money into _____ .

6 Before issuing him with a _____ , the bank checked his credit history.

7 When they went on holiday, they took out travel _____ .

D Study the words in boxes b and c. Make words or phrases used in banking with a word from each box. You can use words more than once.

Example: *key in*

> **b**
>
> key   non   off   on   take   under

> **c**
>
> in   line   out   over   profit   screen
> shore   write

E Match each two-word phrase from Exercise D with a noun or noun phrase from box d.

Example: *non-profit organization*

> **d**
>
> banking   a bond issue   a company
> insurance   investments   organization
> a PIN number   share dealing

F Complete each sentence with one or more of the two-word phrases from Exercise D.

1 In the US, investment banks traditionally guarantee or _____ stock and bond issues.

2 You have to _____ your password before accessing your _____ bank account.

3 _____ share dealing helps you make quick changes to your portfolio.

4 If you don't _____ insurance, it can be costly if your house or car is damaged.

5 Credit unions are _____ organizations, popular in Canada.

6 Investment banks will fund leveraged buyouts when there is a _____ of a company.

7 Many _____ banks are located in areas or jurisdictions of low regulation and taxation.

A Look at the Hadford University handout.

1 What will be in the lecture? Make a list.

2 Write down some key words you expect to hear.

3 Check the pronunciation of the key words, with other students or with a dictionary.

4 How are you going to prepare for this lecture?

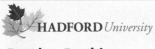

HADFORD *University*

Faculty: Banking

Lecture 3: Banking institutions

B 🎧 Listen to Part 1 of the lecture.

1 What exactly is the lecturer going to talk about? Tick the topic(s) you heard.

the financial services industry   ——

reactions of customers   ——

bank ownership   ——

bank regulations   ——

2 What does the lecturer give definitions of?

3 What do you expect to hear in the next part of the lecture?

C 🎧 Listen to Part 2 of the lecture.

1 What is the main idea of this section?

2 What is another word for merchant bank?

3 What types of thrift banks does the lecturer mention?

4 What three examples does the lecturer give to describe how banks make money?

5 What is a good way to organize notes for this lecture?

Bank of England

D 🎧 Listen to Part 3 of the lecture.

1 How could you write notes for this part?

2 What is the main idea of this section? What are the key words and phrases?

E 🎧 Listen to Part 4 of the lecture.

1 Use your notes to list the main points of the lectures so far.

2 What research must you do now?

F 🎧 Listen and say whether the sentences are true or false. Explain your reasons.

1 ——   3 ——   5 ——

2 ——   4 ——   6 ——

G What do the words in the blue box have in common?

1 Write two sentences for each word using the word as both a verb and a noun.

2 Practise saying each word.

3 Read your sentences to a partner.

4 Does your partner agree with your use of the word? If not, discuss why. Check in a dictionary if you are unsure.

bank deposit fund finance
loan mortgage profit

3.3 Extending skills
stress within words • using information sources • reporting research findings

A 🎧 Listen to some stressed syllables. Identify the word below in each case. Number each word.

Example:

You hear: *1 div* /dɪv/   You write:

broking	___	insurance	___	management	___
capital	___	integration	___	mortgages	___
commission	___	investors	___	profitable	___
conglomerate	___	leveraged	___	subsidiaries	___
dividends	/				

B Where is the main stress in each multi-syllable word in Exercise A?

1 Mark the main stress.

2 Practise saying each word.

C Work in pairs or groups. Define one of the words in Exercise A. The other student(s) must find and say the correct word.

D Make a list of banking services. Categorize the services under the headings in the table.

Borrowing	Saving	General services
credit cards		

E You are going to do some research on a particular lecture topic. You must:

1 find a useful Internet site

2 define your research criteria (e.g., size, income, ownership)

3 define the types of banking institution

Student A
- Do some research on the top five banks in the world.
- Tell your partner about your findings.

Student B
- Do some research on the top American banks.
- Tell your partner about your findings.

Table 1: Top ten banking groups in the world ranked by assets (2004)

Rank 2004	Institution	Total assets (US$ bn.)
1	UBS	1,533
2	Citigroup	1,484
3	Mizuho Financial Group	1,296
4	HSBC Holdings	1,277
5	Crédit Agricole	1,243
6	BNP Paribas	1,234
7	JPMorgan Chase & Co.	1,157
8	Deutsche Bank	1,144
9	Royal Bank of Scotland	1,119
10	Bank of America	1,110

Source: Wikipedia

A You are going to listen to a continuation of the lecture in Lesson 2.

   1 Make a list of points from that lecture.

   2 What is the lecturer going to talk about today? (Clue: You researched it in Lesson 2!)

   3 🎧 Listen to the end of the last lecture again and check your ideas.

B What are the different categories of bank?

   1 Make a list. The opposite page may help you.

   2 🎧 Listen to Part 1 of today's lecture. Make notes on the type of bank and the services offered.

   3 What is the best way to make notes from this lecture? Prepare a page in your notebook.

C 🎧 Listen to Part 2 of the lecture. Make notes.

D 🎧 Listen to Part 3 of the lecture. Make notes.

E Find the logo for each bank on the opposite page. List below the logo the services offered by that bank. Use information from your notes and ask other students.

F 🎧 Listen to the final part of the lecture.

   1 What is the lecturer's conclusion?

   2 Are different services common to different categories of bank?

   3 Do you agree with the lecturer? Discuss your reasons for agreeing or disagreeing.

G Study the prefixes in the table below.

   1 Copy and complete the table by matching each prefix with at least one word from the blue box. Write each complete word in the table.

   2 How does the prefix change the meaning in each case? Check with a dictionary.

   3 Test your partner. Give a meaning. Can your partner guess the word including the prefix?

   Example: *A bank which has not been careful with its loans is at risk of **overexposure**.*

in~	re~	dis~	mis~	over~	under~
				overexposure	

> active   allow   capitalize   charge   count   direct   draw   due   estimate
> exposure   finance   honour   insure   insurer   invest   investment
> manage   pay   sell   solvent   subscribed   sufficient   use   value

HSBC

first direct

ISLAMIC BANK OF BRITAIN
البنك الإسلامي البريطاني

Stress within words

Nouns, **verbs**, **adjectives** and **adverbs** are called **content words** because they carry the meaning.

One-syllable words

Some content words have **one syllable** or sound. This is always stressed.

Examples: 'share, 'text, 'cash

Two-syllable words

Some content words have **two syllables**. Two-syllable nouns and adjectives are often stressed on the first syllable. Two-syllable verbs are often stressed on the second syllable.

Examples:

Nouns	'mortgage, 'balance
Adjectives	'foreign
Verbs	trans'fer, ex'pand

Exceptions:

Nouns	de'mand, a'ccount
Adjectives	u'nique, se'cure
Verbs	'challenge

Multi-syllable words

Some content words have **three or more syllables**. Multi-syllable words are often stressed three syllables from the end.

Example:
Ooo   oOoo   ooOoo

This is true for most words ending in:

~ize/ ~ise	'authorize
~sis	a'nalysis
~ate	'accurate, 'calculate
~ify	'classify, 'specify
~ical	'typical, geo'graphical
~ity	'equity
~ular	par'ticular, 'regular
~ium	'premium
~al	ma'terial, multi'national

Exceptions:
Multi-syllable words ending in the following letters are normally stressed two syllables from the end.

~ic	eco'nomic
~tion	insti'tution, distri'bution
~sion	con'version
~ent	in'solvent, e'fficient

Stress sometimes moves to fit the patterns above when you add a suffix.

Example:
'analyse – a'nalysis

Getting information from other people

From the lecturer

We can sometimes ask a lecturer questions at the end of a lecture. Introduce each question in a polite or tentative way.

Examples:
Could you go over the bit about joint stock banks *again?*
I didn't quite understand what you said about building societies.
I wonder if you could repeat the bank ownership categories, please.
Would you mind giving the definition of an LBO *again?*

From other students

It is a good idea to ask other students after a lecture for information to complete your notes.

Examples:
What did the lecturer say about private banks?
Why did he say that banks can be entrepreneurial?
I didn't get the bit about the difference between a commercial and an investment bank.

Be polite!

It sometimes sounds impolite to ask people a direct question. We often add a polite introduction.

Examples:
Do credit unions operate in the UK?
→ ***Do you know if*** *credit unions operate in the UK?*

What does 'underwrite' mean?
→ ***Can you remember what*** *'underwrite' means?*

Reporting information to other people

We often have to report research findings to a tutor or other students in a seminar. Make sure you can give:
- sources – books, articles, writers, publication dates
- quotes – in the writer's own words
- summary findings – in your own words

4 COMPUTERS IN BANKING

computer jargon • abbreviations and acronyms

A Study the words and phrases in box a.

1 Which words or phrases relate to computers and the Internet? Which relate to books and libraries?

2 Find pairs of words and phrases with similar meanings, one from each group.

3 Check your ideas with the first part of *The Computer Jargon Buster* on the opposite page.

> **a** books browse/search catalogue close cross-reference
> database electronic resources exit/log off hyperlink index
> library log in/log on look up menu open page
> search engine results table of contents web page World Wide Web

B Complete the instructions for using the Learning Resource Centre with words or phrases from box a. Change the form if necessary.

C Study the abbreviations and acronyms in box b.

1 How do you say each one?

2 Divide them into two groups:

● abbreviations

● acronyms

See Vocabulary bank

> **b** CAD CAL CAM DVD HTML
> HTTP ISP LCD PIN ROM URL USB
> WAN WWW

D Test each other on the items in Exercise C.

1 What do the letters stand for in each case?

2 What do they mean?

3 Check your ideas with the second part of *The Computer Jargon Buster* on the opposite page.

E Study the nouns in box c.

1 Make a verb from each noun.

2 Make another noun from the verb.

HADFORD *University*

Learning Resource Centre

Instructions for use:
If you want to access web pages on the
_____ , you must first
_____ to the university Intranet
with your username and password. You can
use any _____ but the default is
Google. _____ for web pages by
typing one or more keywords in the search
box and clicking on **Search**, or pressing
Enter. When the results appear, click on a
_____ (highlighted in blue) to go to
the web page. Click on **Back** to return to the
results listing.
You can also use the university _____
of learning resources. Click on **Banking
Resources** on the main _____ .

> **c** class computer digit
> identity machine

Computer Weekly International magazine

The Computer Jargon Buster

There are many common words used about books and libraries which are translated into jargon words when we talk about using computers and the Internet for similar functions.

books	electronic resources
index	search engine results
cross-reference	hyperlink
catalogue	database
library	World Wide Web
table of contents	menu
look up	browse/search
page	web page
open	log in/log on
close	exit/log off

There are many abbreviations and acronyms in computing. Learn some useful ones.

Abbr./Acr.	What it stands for	What it means
CAD	computer-aided design	using computers to help you design things
CAL	computer-assisted learning	using computers to help you learn
CAM	computer-assisted manufacturing	using computers to help you manufacture things
DVD	digital versatile disk	a disk for storing data, including sound and pictures
HTML	hypertext markup language	a way to write documents so they can be displayed on a website
HTTP	hypertext transfer protocol	a set of rules for transfering files on the WWW, usually included at the beginning of a website address (e.g., http://www. ...)
ISP	Internet service provider	a company that enables access to the Internet
LCD	liquid crystal display	the kind of screen you get on many laptops
PIN	personal identification number	a collection of numbers or letters which are used like a password to identify someone
ROM	read-only memory	a type of permanent computer or disk memory that stores information that can be read or used but not changed
URL	uniform resource locator	a website address, e.g., http://www.garneteducation.com
USB	universal serial bus	a standard way to connect things like printers and scanners to a computer
WAN	wide area network	a way of connecting computers in different places, often very far apart
WWW	World Wide Web	a huge collection of documents that are connected by hypertext links and can be accessed through the Internet

A Discuss these questions.

1 How are computers used in banking today?

2 How has their use in banking changed since the 1970s?

3 How have computers helped banks process and dispense payments?

B Look at the title of the text on the opposite page.

1 What does e-banking stand for?

2 What exactly does it mean ?

3 What would you like to know about it? Make a list of questions.

C One student wrote some ideas about e-banking before reading the text on the opposite page.

1 Write **A** (I agree), **D** (I disagree) or **?** (I'm not sure) next to the ideas on the right.

2 Add any other ideas you have.

D Read all the topic sentences.

1 What is the structure of this text? Choose Structure A or B on the right.

2 What do you expect to find in each paragraph?

E Read the text and check your predictions.

F Answer these questions.

1 What exactly is ACH?

2 How are CHAPS and CHIPS different?

3 Why don't all financial institutions use ACH?

G Topics sometimes develop inside a paragraph.

1 Does the topic develop in each paragraph in the text? If so, underline the word or words which introduce the change.

2 What is the effect of the word or words on the development of the topic?

See Skills bank

E-banking customers can only access their accounts through the Internet. _____

In the 1970s, bank customers did not benefit directly from the computerization of banks. _____

Debit cards have made the processing of payments cheaper. _____

Interbank electronic transfers of funds are computerized. _____

Wholesale funds transfer systems are computerized. _____

All banks use compatible computer hardware and software. _____

_____

_____

_____

Structure A

Para	Contents
1	A definition of e-banking
2	Benefits of banking technology for customers
3	US interbank electronic funds transfer systems
4	Retail funds transfer systems
5	How the retail EFT system operates
6	E-banking problems

Structure B

Para	Contents
1	E-banking in the 21st century
2	Interbank electronic transfers
3	US Federal Reserve computer systems
4	Funds transfer systems
5	Electronic payment systems
6	E-banking impact on banking practices

The development of e-banking

E-BANKING is an umbrella term used by the banking industry. It defines the delivery of banking products and services electronically to financial institutions, individuals or businesses. E-banking customers access accounts, transact business, and obtain financial information via a public or private network, including the Internet. They do this electronically through a personal computer (PC), personal digital assistant (PDA), automated teller machine (ATM), kiosk, or touch-tone telephone.

Electronic transfers between banks were well established by the 1970s, but it was several years before bank customers benefited from computer technology. At first, mainframe computers were used to store huge databases, including customer account information. However, in the early 1980s, personal computers made the computerization of small value processes viable. Thankfully, this took humans out of tedious operations and dramatically affected banking payment systems. Automated teller machines (ATMs) have reduced the need for cashiers and allow customers continuous access to their accounts. Debit cards have reduced the cost of processing payments. Sophisticated databases allow banks to employ new marketing methods.

In the 1970s, the US Federal Reserve System operated a computerized clearing house system, or interbank electronic funds transfer (EFT) system. In comparison, today's high value or wholesale interbank funds transfer systems involve the exchange of very large amounts of money between banks, or participants in the financial markets. SWIFT is the payment transfer system provided and operated by the Society for Worldwide Interbank Financial Telecommunication. Most countries have their own major network or real-time gross settlement (RTGS) system. For example, CHAPS is the UK system, and CHIPS is the US interbank clearing house system.

The retail or bulk funds transfer system handles large-volume, low-value payments, including cheques, credit transfers, direct debits, ATM and EFTPOS transactions. The automated clearing house (ACH) system is generally a domestic electronic clearing system.

Payment via the retail telecommunications network occurs as follows. A consumer sends payment information and authorization to a retailer, who forwards this information electronically to their own bank or ODFI (originating depository financial institution). The ODFI forwards the information to an ACH operator, who sends the transaction information to the consumer's bank or RDFI (receiving depository financial institution) for credit clearance. Once this is gained, the consumer's bank or RDFI makes the funds available by crediting the retailer's account and debiting their client's account. So far, there has been no exchange of funds. The ACH operator now settles the transaction between the ODFI and RDFI (i.e., the retailer's and wholesaler's banks).

Although e-banking has had a significant impact on banking practices, inadequate customer data integration (CDI) is a major problem for banks. Unfortunately, economic considerations determined their selection of the preferred technology for a number of banks. Consequently, these banks have a legacy of computerization systems with hardware from different suppliers, and programs written in an array of different languages – BASIC, PASCAL, etc. However, as CDI requires all software and hardware to be compatible, i.e. able to communicate with each other, it is often not possible to pass certain information between parties.

A Discuss these questions.

   1 You want to find out about computers in banking today. Where would you look for the information? Why?

   2 What keywords would you use to make this search? Why?

B Your search produces 50 results. How can you select the most useful ones without reading all of them? Look at the list of criteria on the right and put a tick or '?'.

C You have some more research tasks (below). Choose up to three keywords or phrases for each search.

   1 What are the issues surrounding wireless technology in banking?

   2 How do I calculate the repayments for a £200 mortgage for a term of 20 years?

   3 Has the euro or the GBP appreciated the most against the USD over the last calendar year?

D Go to a computer and try out your chosen keywords.

> Criteria for choosing to read a result
>
> It contains all of my keywords. ____
>
> The document comes from a journal. ____
>
> It is in the first ten. ____
>
> It has this year's date. ____
>
> It is a large document. ____
>
> The website address ends in .org ____
>
> The website address ends in .edu ____
>
> The website address contains .ac ____
>
> It is a PDF file. ____
>
> It refers to banking. ____
>
> It refers to a person I know (of). ____
>
> It refers to an organization I know (of). ____

A What information is contained in the results listing of a search engine?

   1 Make a list.

   2 Check with the results listings on the opposite page.

B Scan the results listings. Answer these questions.

   1 What keywords were entered?

   2 Why was *journals* used as a keyword? Why is it not in inverted commas?

   3 What happens if you enter *bank* instead of *banking* as a search term?

C Answer these questions.

   1 Which results contain abbreviations or acronyms?

   2 Where is each website address?

   3 Where is the size of each document?

   4 Why are the words in different colours?

   5 Which results have all the keywords?

   6 Which results refer to journals?

   7 Which results come from commercial sites?

   8 What does *similar pages* mean?

   9 What does *cached* mean?

D Continue your research on computers in banking today by entering the keywords into a search engine and accessing three of the results. Compare your findings with other students.

E Choose the most interesting result. Write a paragraph about the information you discovered. Develop the topic within the paragraph with discourse markers and stance markers.

Google

Web   Images   Groups   News   Froogle   Maps   **more »**

Sign in

banking journals + "latest technology"   Search   Advanced Search / Preferences

Web   Results **1 - 10** of about **107,000** for <u>banking</u> <u>journals</u> + <u>latest</u> <u>technology</u> (0.27 sec-

1. <u>Technology News, Industry Research - Computer Business Review</u>
Scotia Capital, Scotiabank's corporate and investment **banking** arm, ... by a European **journal** which suggested that RFID tags could be used to spread viruses. ...
www.cbronline.com/ - 23k - <u>Cached</u> - <u>Similar pages</u>

2. <u>marketing technology - Books, journals, articles @ The Questia ...</u>
Journal article by Chris Jackson; ABA **Banking Journal**, Vol. ... While...using the **latest technology** in your effort...most beneficial marketing tactics. ...
www.questia.com/search/marketing-technology - <u>Similar pages</u>

3. <u>technology for mainstreaming - Books, journals, articles @ The ...</u>
Journal article by Lauren Bielski; ABA **Banking Journal**, Vol. ... for whom the **latest technology** cannot help...helped by technology is even smaller...there. ...
www.questia.com/search/technology-for-mainstreaming - <u>Similar pages</u>

[<u>More results from www.questia.com</u>]

4. <u>Mass High Tech: The **Journal** of New England Technology: New Boston ...</u>
American City Business **Journals** Inc. is the nation's largest publisher of ... the Civil War-era Union Club to consider the **latest technology** business plans. ...
masshightech.bizjournals.com/ masshightech/stories/2006/03/20/story3.html - 32k - <u>Cached</u> - <u>Similar pages</u>

5. <u>Service bureau or in-house? 11 factors to consider. | **Banking** ...</u>
11 factors to consider; from ABA **Banking Journal** covering **Banking**, ... Each choice can result in the "**latest technology**" today and in the future if you ...
www.allbusiness.com/periodicals/article/106943-1.html - 36k - <u>Cached</u> - <u>Similar pages</u>

6. <u>Straight Talk about Internet **Banking**. | **Banking**, Finance and ...</u>
Straight Talk about Internet **Banking** from ABA **Banking Journal** covering **Banking**, ... the first to market -getting up and running with the **latest technology**. ...
www.allbusiness.com/periodicals/article/829814-1.html - 38k - <u>Cached</u> - <u>Similar pages</u>

7. <u>**Banking** on a Standard: IFX for the Retail and Commercial **Banking** ...</u>
The latest **technology** driver to arrive is Web services. ... As an example, a bank customer may log onto his or her online **banking** Web site, which uses IFX, ...
xml.sys-con.com/read/45790.htm - 84k - <u>Cached</u> - <u>Similar pages</u>

8. <u>**Banking** Industry & Financial Market News</u>
The **latest technology** emerging in the **banking** industry is discussed in this ... Ohio State University, Columbus: Department of Finance: **Journal** of Finance ...
www.buzzle.com/chapters/business-and-finance_ news-and-publications_industries-and-market-sectors_**banking**-... - 32k - <u>Cached</u> - <u>Similar pages</u>

9. <u>Finance Magazine Subscriptions</u>
The **Latest Technology** News · IT Stock Quotes and News · Online Games ... ABA **Banking Journal** Covers the commercial **banking** industry in the United States, ...
intelligentedu.tradepub.com/?pt=cat&page=Fi - 108k - <u>Cached</u> - <u>Similar pages</u>

10. <u>BRINT Global Knowledge Network - KM in **banking**</u>
Thumbs up Research Portal on **Banking** and Knowledge Management ... Recommended by Business Week, Fortune, Wall Street **Journal**, Fast Company, ...
https://www.brint.net/forums/showthread.php?t=1051 - 54k - <u>Cached</u> - <u>Similar pages</u>

Common suffixes

Suffixes for verbs

There are some common verb suffixes.

Examples:

~ize	authorize, computerize
~ify	modify, specify, rectify
~ate	authenticate, communicate

When you learn a new noun or adjective, find out how you can make it into a verb.

Suffixes for nouns

There are many suffixes for nouns. But verbs ending in ~ize, ~ify and ~ate form nouns with ~ation.

Examples:

Verb	Noun	
~ize	~ization	authorization, computerization
~ify	~ification	modification, specification
~ate	~ation	authentication, communication

Understanding abbreviations and acronyms

An **abbreviation** is a shorter version of something. For example, PC /piːsiː/ is an abbreviation for *personal computer*.

An **acronym** is similar to an abbreviation, but it is pronounced as a word. For example, CAL /kæl/ is an acronym for *computer-assisted learning*.

We normally write an abbreviation or acronym with **capital letters**, although the full words have lower case letters.

We **pronounce** the vowel letters in **abbreviations** in this way:

A	/eɪ/
E	/iː/
I	/aɪ/
O	/əʊ/
U	/juː/

We normally **pronounce** the vowel letters in **acronyms** in this way:

A	/æ/
E	/e/
I	/ɪ/
O	/ɒ/
U	/ʌ/

Developing ideas in a paragraph

Introducing the topic

In a text a **new paragraph** indicates the start of **a new topic**.

The topic is given in the **topic sentence** which is at or near the beginning of the paragraph. The topic sentence gives the topic, and also makes a comment about the topic.

Example:
E-banking is an umbrella term used in the banking industry.

The **topic** is *e-banking*. The **comment** is *this is an umbrella term*.

The sentences that follow then expand or explain the topic sentence.

Example:
It defines the delivery of banking products and services electronically …

Developing the topic

A paragraph is normally about the same basic topic (the 'unity principle'). However, within a paragraph, ideas often **develop** beyond the comment. This development is often shown by
- a discourse marker: *but, although,* etc.
- a stance marker: *thankfully, unfortunately,* etc.

Discourse markers generally make a connection between the previous information and what comes next. They mainly introduce **contrasts** or **additional information**.

Example:
Electronic transfers between banks were well established by the 1970s …
***However**, in the early 1980s, personal computers made the computerization of small value processes viable.*

Stance markers show the writer's point of view or attitude to the information, i.e., whether he/she is surprised, pleased, unhappy, etc. about the information.

Example:
***Thankfully**, this took humans out of tedious operations …*

Recording and reporting findings

When you do research, record information about the source. You must refer to the source when you report your findings.

Examples:
According to Heffernan in her book Modern Banking (2005), …
As Sethi says in his 2005 article in The Journal of Business Ethics, …
Johnson (2005) states that …

You should give the full information about the source in your reference list or bibliography. For more information about this, see Unit 10 *Skills bank*.

5 BANK PERFORMANCE

A Study Figure 1 and Table 1 on the opposite page.

1 Where would you find this type of information?

2 Who is it written for?

B Study the words in box a.

1 What part of speech is each word?

2 Find pairs of opposites.

3 Which pairs relate to which words in box b?

C Study Figure 1 on the opposite page.

1 What do the blue bars show?

2 What is the horizontal scale?

3 What items are on the left of the line?

4 What items are on the right?

D Study Table 1 on the opposite page.

1 What happened to performance in 2007?

2 Complete Table 1 with information from Figure 1. Use numbers from box c. Not all the numbers are used. Some may be used twice.

E Study the text on the right, which describes Table 1.

1 Complete the first paragraph with a preposition in each space.

2 Complete the second paragraph with one or two words in each space.

F Study Table 1 again. Discuss these questions.

1 What happened to the doubtful debts provision in 2007?

2 Why might interest expenses grow by 5.6% whereas interest income grows by only 4.4%?

3 What happened to other banking income in 2007? How might you explain this?

4 The annual inflation rate was 3.4%. How therefore would you explain an increase in personnel costs of 6.5%?

5 Occupancy-related costs increased by 10.4%. Why?

G Discuss the changes shown in Table 1. Use a variety of nouns, verbs, adjectives and adverbs.

---

a

assets   deficit   distributed   expenses   income   intangible   liabilities   loss   non-operating   operating   profit   retained   surplus   tangible

b

account   assets   profits   revenue

c

17,780	11,890	–3,015	10.4
4.4	–2,815	4,385	3.7
2.3	–1,315	4,450	18.8
3.9	–27.6	3,182	

Table 1 shows changes _____ the bank's financial performance _____ the years 2006 and 2007. There was an increase _____ 4.4% _____ net profit _____ the year 2006.

While there was a _____ of 10.4% in occupancy-related expenses, the provision for doubtful debts _____ by 27.6%. Other banking income showed a/an _____ of 6.3% from the previous year. Interest income also _____ to $18,560m, a/an _____ of 4.4%. However, personnel expenses also _____ .

ANW Bank plc
Annual Review and Summary

Consolidated Financial Statements — Summary

The following is a summary of the information which appears in the full annual report and accounts. For further information, please consult the full annual report on our website, or request a free copy from the address on the back cover.

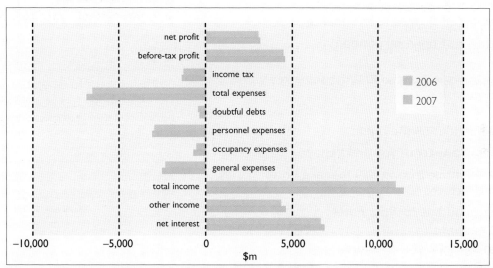

Figure 1 *ANW Bank — Financial performance 2006 and 2007*

	2007 $m	2006 $m	% change
Interest income	18,560		4.4
Interest expenses	−11,890	−11,260	5.6
Net interest income	6,670	6,520	
Other banking income	4,730		6.3
Total income	**11,400**	**10,970**	
Personnel expenses	−3,210		6.5
Occupancy expenses	−530	−480	
General expenses	−2,815	−2,710	3.9
Provision for doubtful debts	−275	−380	
Total expenses	**−6,830**	**−6,585**	3.7
Before-tax profit	4,570		4.2
Income tax	−1,364		
Net profit	**3,206**	**3,070**	

Table 1 *ANW Bank — Statement of financial performance for the year ended 31st March 2007*

A You are going to hear a lecture on assessing a bank's financial strength.

   1 Look at the handout. What will the lecturer talk about? Make a list of points.

   2 Put your points in a logical order.

B 🎧 Listen to Part 1 of the lecture. How will the lecture be organized? Number these topics.

   • assets   ____

   • equity   ____

   • liabilities   ____

   • statement of financial performance   ____

   • statement of financial position   ____

C Study the topics in Exercise B. Write some key words for each one.

D Read the handout on the right.

   1 Highlight any terms you don't know.

   2 What might be a good way to make notes for this lecture?

   3 Make an outline for your notes.

E 🎧 Listen to Part 2 of the lecture.

   1 Add information to your outline notes.

   2 Which of the topics in Exercise B are discussed?

   3 What are normally the largest assets held by the bank?

F 🎧 Listen to Part 3 of the lecture. Make notes.

   1 Which topic in Exercise B is mentioned?

   2 What is the largest liability for the bank?

   3 Which topic mentioned was *not* in the outline?

   4 What is the lecturer talking about when she loses her place?

   5 What do banks make financial provisions for?

🍁 HADFORD *University*

Faculty: Banking

Lecture 5: Assessing a bank's financial strength

Table 1: *A financial statement*

ANW Bank

**Statement of financial position
as at 31st March 2007**

	2007 $m	2006 $m
Assets		
Cash and liquid assets	6,540	6,250
Due from other financial institutions	17,445	18,635
Trading securities	24,570	23,320
Investments and securities	9,625	9,255
Loans and advances	166,885	158,750
Property, plant and equipment	6,450	5,660
Total assets	231,515	221,870
Liabilities		
Due to other financial institutions	32,680	29,755
Deposits and other borrowings	148,665	144,790
Income tax liabilities	1,680	1,375
Provisions	2,800	2,500
Bonds, notes and subordinated debt	28,780	26,925
Total liabilities	214,605	205,345
Net assets	16,910	16,525
Equity		
Contributed equity	10,000	10,000
Reserves	1,100	1,000
Retained profits	5,810	5,525
Total equity	16,910	16,525

G The lecturer used these words and phrases. Match synonyms.

1	analysis	easy to understand
2	modify	examination
3	provisions	allowances
4	requirements	regulations
5	self-explanatory	depending on
6	subject to	change

5.3 Extending skills
note-taking symbols • stress within words • lecture language

A Look at a student's notes from the lecture in Lesson 2.

1 What do the symbols and abbreviations mean?

2 The notes contain some mistakes. Find and correct them.

3 Make the corrected notes into a spidergram.

4 What do you expect the next part of the lecture to be about?

B 🎧 Listen to the final part of the lecture.

1 Complete your notes.

2 Check your notes with the handout in Lesson 2. Make changes as necessary.

3 Why does the lecturer have to stop?

4 What is the research task?

> <u>Assess strength</u>
>
> <u>Comparative analysis</u>
> - cf. other banks
> - indiv. bank cf. prev. yrs.
> 1 State. fin. perf. = 12 mths.
> 2 " " position = @ certain date
> what bank owns must = what bank owes
> i.e. assets = liabilities + capital
> 2.1 Assets NB loans to cust. = largest liab.
> 2.2 Equity – largest = gen. deposits & other borrowings

C 🎧 Listen to some stressed syllables. Identify the word below in each case. Number each word.

Example: You hear: *1 pa* /pæ/   You write:

accumulated	___	contributed	___	preceded	___
analysis	___	equation	___	regime	___
arguably	___	equity	___	retained	___
comparative	_1_	generally	___	securities	___

D Study part of the lecture on the right.

1 Choose the best word or phrase in each case.

2 🎧 Listen and check your ideas.

3 Match words or phrases from the blue box with each word or phrase. There may be more than one option.

4 Think of other words or phrases with similar meanings.

> generally   in essence   in fact
> in other words   lastly   possibly
> practically   probably
> some people say   that is to say
> therefore   usually

E Discuss the research task set by the lecturer.

1 What kind of information should you find?

2 What do you already know?

3 Where can you find more information?

> Negotiable financial instruments are *basically / arguably* financial instruments that can be assigned to another purchaser at any time. *Therefore / What I mean is*, for example, government bonds purchased by the bank.
>
> Financial instruments held for the long term are included under 'Investments and securities'. *Usually / Arguably*, they could be included in a financial instruments category. *It follows that / In other words*, the bank's shares in listed companies are included under 'Investments and securities'.
>
> *Actually / Naturally*, the largest type of assets held by a bank is *normally / on the other hand* loans and advances made to bank customers, which is the next category.
>
> And *in the end / finally*, we have the fixed assets held by the bank. These are fundamentally the 'Property, plant and equipment' owned by the bank.

A Study the diagram at the top of the opposite page.

   1 What do we call this kind of diagram?

   2 What does it show?

B 🎧 Listen to some extracts from a seminar about the capital adequacy ratio.

   1 What is wrong with the contribution of the last speaker in each case? Choose from the following:

- it is irrelevant
- the student interrupts
- the student doesn't contribute anything to the discussion
- it is not polite
- the student doesn't explain the relevance

   2 What exactly does the student say, in each case?

   3 What should the student say or do, in each case?

C 🎧 Listen to some more extracts from the same seminar.

   1 How does the second speaker make an effective contribution in each case? Choose from the following:

- by making clear how the point is relevant
- by bringing in another speaker
- by asking for clarification
- by paraphrasing to check understanding
- by giving specific examples to help explain a point

   2 What exactly does the student say, in each case?

   3 What other ways do you know of saying the same things?

D Make a table of **Do's** (helpful ways) and **Don'ts** (unhelpful ways) of contributing to seminar discussions.

Do's	Don'ts
ask politely for information	demand information from other students

E Work in groups. The teacher will ask you to study one of three graphs.

- Group A: look at the graph showing **Assets** on the opposite page.
- Group B: look at the graph showing **Liabilities** on page 103.
- Group C: look at the graph showing **Equity** on page 104.

   1 Think of different ways to describe the changes. Take turns.

   2 Make notes summarizing the information.

F Form new groups. Each group must have at least one person who studied each graph.

   1 Report on your findings. Listen to the findings of other people.

   2 Use your notes to report on your discussion in a class seminar. Decide if the bank was in a better or worse financial position in 2007 than in 2006.

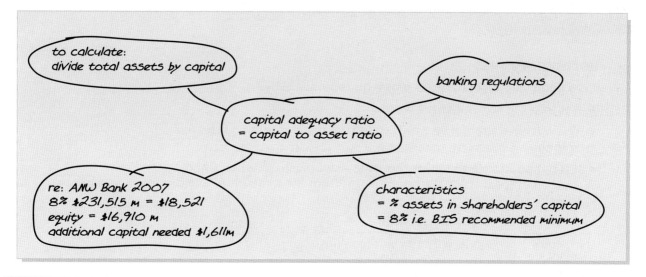

to calculate:
divide total assets by capital

banking regulations

capital adequacy ratio
= capital to asset ratio

re: ANW Bank 2007
8% $231,515 m = $18,521
equity = $16,910 m
additional capital needed $1,611m

characteristics
= % assets in shareholders' capital
= 8% i.e. BIS recommended minimum

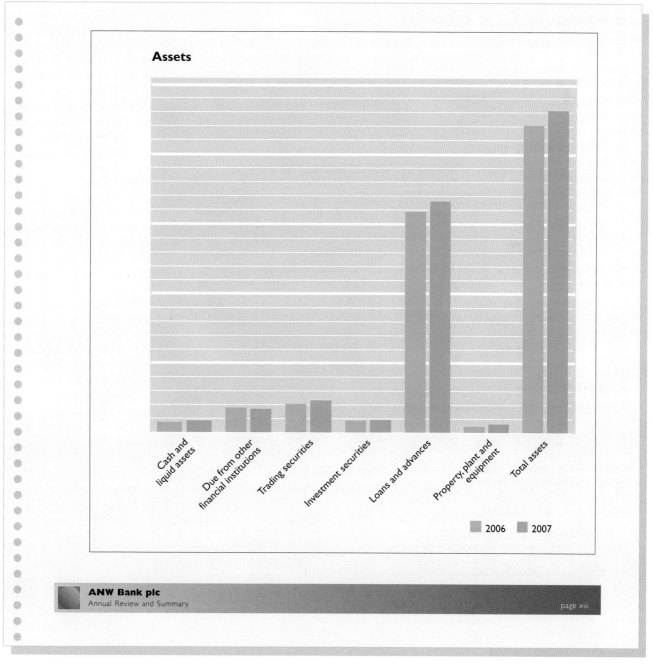

Assets

Cash and liquid assets · Due from other financial institutions · Trading securities · Investment securities · Loans and advances · Property, plant and equipment · Total assets

2006　2007

ANW Bank plc
Annual Review and Summary

Vocabulary sets

It is a good idea to learn words which go together. Why?

- It is easier to remember the words.
- You will have alternative words to use when paraphrasing research findings.
- It is not good style to repeat the same word often, so writers, and sometimes speakers, make use of words from the same set to avoid repetition.

You can create a vocabulary set with:

synonyms	words with similar meanings, e.g., *previous/prior*
antonyms	words with opposite meanings, e.g., *profit/loss*
hypernyms	a general word for a set of words, e.g., *money = coins, notes, cheques*
linked words	e.g., *banking, depositors, customers, accounts*

Describing trends

You can use a variety of phrases to discuss trends and statistics.

Examples:

Go up	No change	Go down	Adverbs
rise *increase* *grow* *improve* *soar*	*stay the same* *remain at …* *doesn't change* *is unchanged*	*fall* *decrease* *decline* *worsen* *drop* *plunge* *plummet*	*slightly* *gradually* *steadily* *significantly* *sharply* *dramatically*

Stance

Speakers often use certain words and phrases to show how they feel about what they are saying. Common stance words are:

adverbs	*arguably* *naturally* *sadly*
phrases	*of course, …* *it's essential to/that …* *we might say that …*

In many cases, different stance words and phrases are used in spoken and written language.

Spoken	Written
another thing	*additionally*
it seems	*evidently*
unfortunately	*regrettably*
believe	*contend*

Signpost language in a lecture

At the beginning of a lecture, a speaker will usually outline the talk. To help listeners understand the order of topics, the speaker will use phrases such as:

To start with, I'll talk about …
Then I'll discuss …
After that, we'll look at …
I'll finish by giving a summary of …

During the lecture, the speaker may:

indicate a new topic	*Moving on (from this) …*
say the same thing in a different way	*What I mean is, …* *That is to say, …* *To put it another way, …*
return to the main point	*Where was I? Oh, yes.* *To return to the main point …* *As I was saying …*

Seminar language

The discussion leader may:

ask for information	*What did you learn about …?* *Can you explain …?* *Can you tell me a bit more about …?*
ask for opinions	*What do you make of …?* *This is interesting, isn't it?*
bring in other speakers	*What do you think, Liz?*

Participants should:

be polite when disagreeing	*Actually, I don't quite agree …*
make relevant contributions	*That reminds me …*
give examples to explain a point	*I can give an example of that.*

Participants may:

ask for clarification	*Could you say more about …?*
paraphrase to check understanding	*So what you're saying is …*
refer back to establish relevance	*Just going back to …*

6.1 Vocabulary paraphrasing at sentence level

A Study the words in Table 1.

1 What is the meaning of each word in general English?

2 What is the meaning of each word in banking?

3 Identify the part of speech of the word in banking.

4 Find a synonym for each word. (Some may not be possible.)

B Study the table on the opposite page. Discuss these questions.

1 What does the table show?

2 Which country or area does each central bank represent?

3 Is there a common objective across all banks? If so, what is it?

C Study the highlighted words in the table on the opposite page. Complete Table 2.

1 What part of speech is each word?

2 What is the meaning of each word in banking?

3 Find a synonym (a word or a phrase) for each word.

D Study the words in Table 3 on this page.

1 What is the base word in each case?

2 What part of speech is each base word?

3 Add a prefix to make an antonym for each word.

E Student A has written about the role and function of central banks. Look at his notes on the opposite page.

1 There are some mistakes in the notes. Say whether each sentence is true or false.

2 Rewrite the false sentences so that they are true.

F Look at Student B's notes on the opposite page.

1 Complete the notes using the appropriate form of the verb in the brackets.

2 Write a paraphrase of each sentence.

See Vocabulary bank

Federal Reserve, Washington, D.C.

Table 1

Word	Banking meaning	Part of speech	Synonym
appreciate	increase in value	v	increase
basket			
capital			
reserves			
stable			
stock			

Table 2

Word	Part of speech	Banking meaning	Synonym
mandate			
stability			
prejudice			
maintenance			
support			
quantified			
prioritization			
qualitative			
sound			
specification			

Table 3

Word	Base word	Part of speech	Antonym with prefix
stability			
quantified			
employment			
sound			

Central banks

The mandate of central banks in the euro area, the UK, the USA and Japan

	European Central Bank	Bank of England	Federal Reserve System	Bank of Japan
Objectives	▪ low inflation ▪ monetary stability ▪ without prejudice to low inflation, support of the general economic policies of the Community	▪ low inflation ▪ monetary stability ▪ subject to monetary stability, support of the economic policy of the government, including its objectives for growth and employment	▪ low inflation ▪ maximum employment ▪ moderate long-term interest rates	▪ keep inflation low ▪ monetary stability contributing to the sound development of the national economy
Primary objective	maintenance of low inflation	maintenance of low inflation	no prioritization	maintenance of low inflation
Specification of the inflation objective	quantified by the ECB	quantified by the Treasury	qualitative specification provided by the Federal Reserve	qualitative specification provided by the Bank of Japan

Source: ECB Monthly Bulletin Nov 2002

Student A

1 The main objective of the Federal Reserve System is maintaining low inflation.

2 The US government sets the inflation policy of the Federal Reserve System.

3 The goal of the Bank of Japan is to maintain low inflation.

4 The Bank of England is the only central bank that does not specify its own inflation objective.

5 The government of Japan oversees the inflation policy.

6 It is the mandate of the European Central Bank to support the economic policies of the European Union at all times.

Student B

1 The Bank of England's primary goal is _____ (maintain) low inflation.

2 The Bank's objectives for inflation _____ (quantify) by the Treasury.

3 Support for its growth and employment objectives _____ (require) by the government.

4 The Bank of England's objectives of low inflation, and growth and employment _____ (conflict).

A Discuss these questions.

   1 Who are the owners of a central bank?

   2 What are the main functions of a central bank?

   3 Explain the term 'lender of last resort'.

B Look at the title, the introduction and the first sentence of each paragraph on the opposite page.

   1 What will the text be about?

   2 Using your ideas from this exercise and from Exercise A above, write some research questions.

The Bank of Japan, Tokyo

C Read the text. Does it answer your questions?

D Study the highlighted sentences in the text. Find and underline the subject, verb and object or complement in each sentence. **See *Skills bank***

E Two students paraphrased a paragraph of the text.

   1 Which paragraph is it?

   2 Which paraphrase is better? Why?

Student A

> The objective for most central banks is to carry out policies that result in a stable currency and economy.
>
> By setting the official interest rate of their country, central banks hope to manage the inflation rate.
>
> Inflation involves an increase in the price of a 'basket' of goods rather than an increase in just one product or service.

Student B

> The majority of state banks have to execute the agreed financial goals of parliament.
>
> A certain number of them fix the government interest rate.
>
> This is seen as a means of controlling inflation (increasing costs on a range of products), and deflation.

F Read the text on the opposite page.

   1 Select part of the text.

   2 Paraphrase it in your own words without changing the meaning:

     ● use synonyms where possible

     ● change from active to passive voice as necessary

     ● use a replacement subject where possible

   3 Exchange your paraphrase with another student or pair. Can you identify the part of the text they selected?

   See *Vocabulary bank*

The role of the central bank

A central bank (reserve bank or monetary authority) is created by government legislation. It normally has the legal right to create money. It can print more money to increase the supply, or exchange money for securities. It can sell securities to decrease the money supply. It is responsible for maintaining stability in the banking system of its country, or group of member states. In times of financial crisis, the central bank acts as 'lender of last resort' (i.e., extending credit when no one else will) to the banking sector. Some central banks, such as the Bank of England, are involved in coordinating, with solvent banks, 'lifeboat' rescues of banks in crisis.

The mandate of most central banks is to carry out their government's fiscal and monetary policy to ensure a stable economy and currency. Some central banks set their country's official interest rate. They do this to manage inflation (a rise in the price of a 'basket' of goods), as well as deflation. Central banks can influence money supply, interest rates, and foreign exchange rates. They may also manage the country's foreign exchange, gold reserves, plus the government's stock register.

Central bank structures and conditions vary significantly within and across nations. The European Central Bank (ECB) operates across several countries. The Federal Reserve Bank (Fed) operates across all states in the USA. Central banks are managed by a board of directors. The head of the central bank is usually a governor or president. All governments have some influence over their central banks. In the USA, the chairman of the Federal Reserve Bank is appointed by the president. However, his or her appointment must be confirmed by Congress. In some countries, the key monetary policy decisions are made by committees or individuals, independent of the political appointee. The Monetary Policy Committee of the Bank of England, for example, is dominated by representatives of private corporations.

In most countries, a central bank carries out supervision and regulation of the banking industry. Some central banks still require trading banks to maintain a certain amount of their deposits as reserves. However, most central banks address credit risk by requiring trading banks to meet certain capital requirements. These requirements (called capital adequacy ratios) require banks to hold a percentage of their assets as capital. The Basel Capital Accord's current guideline is 8% for international banks. This means that when a bank reaches its lending limit, 92% of assets, it must raise additional capital if it wishes to continue to increase its lending.

Central banks may also provide financial services such as transfer of funds, banknotes and coins or foreign currency. The Bank of Japan, for example, is a central bank that is actively engaged in financial transactions with other financial institutions. In this role, the central bank is known as the 'bank of banks'. In some countries, this may be the responsibility of a government department such as the ministry of finance.

Most central banks are state-owned. However, many economists view government intervention in the monetary policy of the country as undesirable. Advocates of an independent central bank argue that the power to create money, and the power to spend it (e.g., funding government budgets), should be separate. Independence, it is argued, creates a more credible monetary policy. Consequently, the financial market reacts more in line with the direction indicated by the central bank. It is also argued that political interference or pressure may lead to 'boom and bust' economic cycles as governments attempt to manipulate the economy before an election for short-term political gain. This may result in higher employment and consumer spending, but lead to higher inflation in the long term. During the 1990s, many countries, influenced by research correlating central bank independence with low and stable inflation, increased central bank independence. Critics of this trend say independence can weaken the central bank's public accountability. They argue that central bank independence needs to be balanced with accountability to the public and their elected representatives.

A Study the words in box a.

   1 What part of speech is each word?

   2 Think of a word or phrase with a similar meaning to each word.

a

about   data   graph
period   rates   relationship
represents

B Study the words in box b.

   1 What is the base word in each case?

   2 What is its meaning?

   3 How does the affix change the part of speech?

b

clustered   correlated
independence   rated   significantly
subsequently   targeting

C Study Figure 1 and the summary at the bottom of this page.
Complete the summary with words from Exercises A and B.

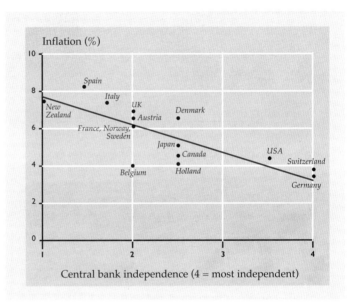

D Study the highlighted sentences in the summary.

   1 Identify the main subject, verb and object.

   2 Rewrite the first sentence as passive.

E Study the highlighted sentences again. Identify the dependent clauses.

   1 How are the clauses linked to the main part of the sentence?

   2 What does each word at the beginning of the dependent clause refer to?

Figure 1: *Central bank independence and inflation 1955–1988*

   3 Make the clauses into complete sentences.

Figure 1, which _____ the _____ 1955 to 1988, shows the _____ between central bank _____ and inflation. Inflation _____ were averaged over the 33 years then _____ to an index of central bank independence. Bank independence was _____ on a scale of 1 to 4. The least independent central bank was rated 1 whereas the most independent was rated 4.

   If you look at the red line, you will see that the USA, Switzerland and Germany are _____ around 4 on the independence _____ . They all have _____ 4% inflation. When you look at New Zealand, you will see it has 8% inflation, as well as being the least independent. Although Spain has just over 8% inflation, it scores about 1.5 on the central bank independence scale. What the _____ indicates is that there is a positive correlation, for the period represented on the _____ , between central bank independence and low inflation. However, for countries whose central banks _____ adopted inflation _____ , the data shown has changed _____ .

6.4 Extending skills · writing complex sentences

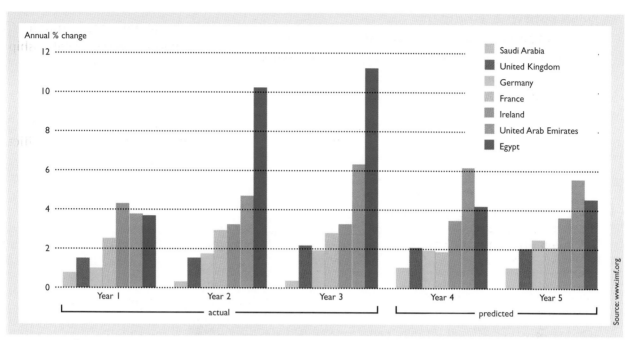

Figure 2: *Inflation rates – Middle East and Europe*

A Study Figure 2. Discuss the following questions.

1 What does the graph show?
2 What interesting statistics can you find?
3 Does your own country appear on the graph?

B Study the sentences on the right.

1 Make one sentence from the sentences in each box, using the method given in red. Include the words in blue.
2 Write all the sentences as one paragraph.

C Study Figure 2.

1 Select two countries to compare.
2 In your own words, write a paragraph comparing them. Call the two countries A and B.
3 Swap paragraphs with a partner.
4 Identify the countries your partner selected on the graph.

Saudi Arabia has generally low inflation.
Saudi Arabia had an inflation rate below 1%.

relative   In the first three years

Economists predict that inflation will remain stable.
Economists predict an inflation rate around 1%.

passive, ellipsis   during years 4 and 5

Saudi Arabia has huge exports of petrochemicals.
Saudi Arabia has accumulated large dollar reserves.

passive   as a result

They are able to import items cheaply.
This means there is no inflationary impact on their economy.

participle   In addition

Reporting findings

You cannot use another writer's words unless you directly quote. Instead, you must restate or **paraphrase**.

There are several useful ways to do this:

use a synonym of a word or phrase	costs ➔ expenses most countries ➔ the majority of nations
change negative to positive and vice versa	sales declined ➔ sales didn't increase
use a replacement subject	interest rates may decline ➔ there may be a decline in interest rates
change from active to passive or vice versa	the reserve bank can print more money ➔ more money can be printed
change the order of information	in other countries this may be the responsibility of a government department ➔ government departments may have this responsibility in other countries

When reporting findings from one source, you should use all the methods above.

Example:

Original text	Advocates of an independent central bank argue that the power to create money and the power to spend it (e.g., funding government budgets) should be separate.
Report	The claimed advantages of bank independence are the separation of interests between the money supply side and the government expenditure side of monetary policy.

Important

When paraphrasing, you should aim to make sure that 90% of the words you use are different from the original. It is not enough to change only a few vocabulary items: this will result in plagiarism.

Example:

Original text	It can sell securities to decrease money supply.
Plagiarism	It can sell investments to reduce money supply.

Finding the main information

Sentences in academic and technical texts are often very long.

Example:
During the 1990s, many countries, influenced by research correlating central bank independence with low and stable inflation, increased central bank independence.

You often don't have to understand every word but you must **identify the subject, the verb and the object**, if there is one.

For example, in the sentence above, we find:
subject = *countries*
verb = *increased*
object = *independence*

Remember!

You can remove any leading prepositional phrases at this point to help you find the subject, e.g., *During the 1990s …*

You must then find **the main words which modify** the subject, the verb and the object or complement.

In the sentence above we find:
Which countries? = many countries
What increased? = central bank independence
Why independence? = influenced by research

Ellipsis

Sometimes, if the meaning is clear, words are implied rather than actually given in the text.

Example:
In this (financial services) *role the central bank is known as the 'bank of banks'.*

7 INTERNATIONAL BANKING

7.1 Vocabulary — compound nouns • fixed phrases

A Study the words in box a.

1 Match nouns in column 1 with nouns in column 2 to make compound nouns.

2 Which word in each phrase has the stronger stress?

B Study the phrases in box b.

1 Complete each phrase with one word.

2 Is each phrase followed by:
- a noun (including gerund)?
- subject + verb?
- an infinitive?

3 How is each phrase used?

C Look at the pictures on the opposite page showing the international trade and finance cycle. What happens at each stage?

D Look at the extracts from a leaflet on the right.

1 Read the sentences carefully.

2 Match each extract (A–F) with a picture on the opposite page.

3 Complete each sentence with a phrase from box b. You can use one phrase twice.

E Complete the Hadford University handout below using phrases from box c.

a	1	2
	credit exchange	instruments lines
	export financial	margin market
	guide payment	rate stability
	political profit	terms worthy

b

as shown ...   as well ...   in addition ...
in order ...   in such a way ...   in the case ...
known ...   the end ...   the use ...

International trade using open account terms

Ⓐ Nesi International then distributes the computers to domestic retailers. April 20th marks _____ the cycle for this order with the receipt of payment by Nesi International from the domestic retailers.

Ⓑ A sales contract for 40 computers is signed between Nesi International, Hong Kong and Rainbow Corporation, Singapore (formerly _____ Rainbow Computer Corporation) on February 1st.

Ⓒ Rainbow Corporation ships the computers to Nesi International in Hong Kong. _____ minimize costs, the computers are sent by sea.

Ⓓ At _____ the checking process, Nesi International authorizes its bank to make payment to Rainbow Corporation's bank under open account terms.
(_____ open account terms, because they offer the least security to the exporter, is only advisable _____ an importer who is well known to and trusted by the exporter.)

Ⓔ Nesi International checks the order to make sure it is correct. _____ , the computers are checked to make sure they are not damaged.

Ⓕ Rainbow Corporation buys computer chips from Letni Corporation in Japan _____ motherboards from India to complete the order.

🍁 **HADFORD** *University*

There are _____ factors to _____ when deciding payment terms. For example, the relationship between the seller and purchaser.

_____ the bank, there is less financial risk where there is a strong trading partnership _____ trust and integrity. _____ other factors influence risk, including the type of goods and the distance travelled. A shipment of perishable goods, if delayed, could mean the bank has to _____ payment disputes and _____ establish whose liability it is. _____ economic or political problems in either country would also indicate potential financing risks.

c

a number of   a variety of
at the same time
bear in mind   based on   deal with
from the point of view of
the beginning of
the development of

54

A Look at the slide on the right. Write three questions you would like the lecture to answer.

International banking
(Lecture 1)

HADFORD *University*

Lecture overview

- The international trade process
- International trade finance
- The role of banks

B 🎧 Listen to Part 1 of the lecture.

1 What is the lecturer going to talk about today? Write *yes, no* or *not given*.

international regulations _____

international trade finance _____

credibility of banks _____

payment options _____

currency fluctuations _____

2 What does *payment terms* mean?

C 🎧 Listen to Part 2 of the lecture.

1 Make notes.

2 What are two other words for *purchaser* in international trade?

3 What four methods of payment in international trade are mentioned?

4 Were your questions in Exercise A answered?

D Match each phrase (1–8) in the table on the right with the type of information that can follow.

E 🎧 Listen to Part 3 of the lecture.

1 Makes notes on the information that comes after the phrases in Exercise D.

2 Were your questions in Exercise A answered?

Fixed phrase	Followed by ...
1 An important concept (is) ...	a different way to think about the topic
2 What do I mean by ...?	an imaginary example
3 In financial terms, ...	a new idea or topic that the lecturer wants to discuss
4 Say ...	a comment about something visual (e.g., a diagram or lecture slide) OR a fact that has just been demonstrated
5 In this way ...	a general idea put into a financial context
6 Looking at it another way, ...	a key statement or idea
7 As you can see, ...	an explanation of a word or phrase
8 The point is ...	a concluding comment giving a result of something

F 🎧 Listen for sentences 1–4 in Part 4 of the lecture. Which sentence (**a** or **b**) follows in each case? Why?

1 The payment form most beneficial to the exporter is cash with order.
   a With this type of payment, the importer pays for the goods pre-shipment.
   b The importer pays for the goods pre-shipment with this type of payment.

2 A letter of credit is the most common form of payment used in international trade.
   a In this situation, the importer raises the letter of credit at the request of the exporter.
   b The importer raises the letter of credit at the request of the exporter in this situation.

3 Documentary collection offers less security than a letter of credit.
   a In this case, a bill of exchange is raised by the exporter and signed by the importer.
   b What happens here is the exporter's bank receives payment, or a bill of exchange, against the shipping documents.

4 Cash on delivery terms are used only when the exporter is confident that there is no risk involved.
   a Under these terms, the exporter ships the goods and sends the commercial documents directly to the buyer.
   b What's different to the previous options is that the exporter ships the goods and sends the commercial documents directly to the buyer.

G This lecturer is not very well organized. What problems are there in the lecture?

7.3 Extending skills
stress within words • fixed phrases • giving sentences a special focus

A 🎧 Listen to some stressed syllables. Identify the word below in each case. Number each word.

Example:

You hear: *1 op* /op/   You write:

contributing	_____	exchange	_____	irrevocable	_____
criteria	_____	financial	_____	merchandise	_____
decision	_____	fluctuation	_____	optimal	_1_
depreciation	_____	instability	_____	significant	_____

B Study the diagrams on the right.

  1 Complete the diagrams with arrows and stage numbers.

  2 🎧 Listen again to two extracts from the lecture in Lesson 2 and check your ideas.

  3 Describe one of the flowcharts to your partner.

C Rewrite these sentences to give a special focus. Begin with the words in brackets.

  1 Cash with order terms are the most beneficial for the exporter. (*It*)

  2 The letter of credit is the most common payment used in international trade. (*It*)

  3 With cash on delivery it is important that the exporter and the importer have a relationship of trust. (*What*)

  4 A bill of exchange is raised by the exporter and signed by the importer as payment is not received until after delivery of the goods. (*The reason*)

D 🎧 Listen to the final part of the lecture.

  1 What is the main idea of this part?

  2 What research task(s) are you asked to do?

E Study the phrases from the lecture in box a.
For which of the following purposes did the lecturer use each phrase?

  - to introduce a new topic
  - to make a major point
  - to add points
  - to finish a list
  - to give an example
  - to restate

See *Vocabulary bank* and *Skills bank*

F Choose one section of the lecture. Refer to your notes and give a spoken summary. Use the fixed phrases and ways of giving special focus that you have looked at.

G Work with a partner.

  1 Make a flowchart for an activity, project or process.

  2 Present your chart to another pair. Practise using fixed phrases and ways of giving special focus.

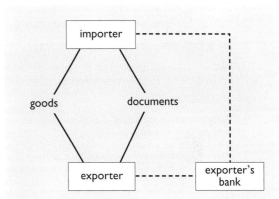

Figure 1: *Cash with order*

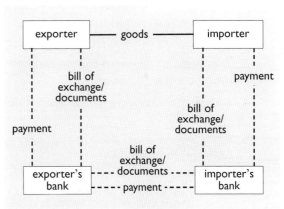

Figure 2: *Documentary collection*

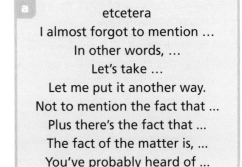

a	
	etcetera
	I almost forgot to mention …
	In other words, …
	Let's take …
	Let me put it another way.
	Not to mention the fact that …
	Plus there's the fact that …
	The fact of the matter is, …
	You've probably heard of …

A Look at the map on the opposite page.

1 What does it show?

2 Where is the company located?

3 Where does the information come from?

B Work in groups. Answer the following questions about Rainbow Corporation's new markets using your world knowledge.

1 Which is the least stable economically?

2 Which is most at risk from currency devaluation?

3 Which supply route is the longest?

C 🎧 Listen to the first extract from a seminar about export orders.

1 Why has the company decided to expand its international markets?

2 Why has the company approached the bank?

D 🎧 Listen to Extract 2 of the seminar. Are these statements true or false?

1 In Indonesia, the legal processes for recovery of payment are good. _____

2 The Mexican order is from a new client. _____

3 The terms of payment should not be based on one factor only. _____

4 An importer can pay for goods not yet manufactured. _____

5 Costs are the main issue in choosing optimal financing terms. _____

E Study the uses in box a and the phrases in box b.

1 Write A, B, C or D next to each phrase to show its use.

2 🎧 Listen to Part 2 again to check your answers.

F Work in groups of four. As a group, choose one of the following countries:

• Belgium   • New Zealand   • Mexico

The aim is to research the optimal financing option for your country and situation.

1 Read the case study information on the opposite page.

2 Look at the assignment on the right and locate your payment terms information. Make brief notes.

3 Report back orally to your group. Use fixed phrases to ask for and give clarification.

4 As a group, reach a consensus on the best financing option.

5 Report to the class on your discussion, giving reasons for your decisions.

---

a

A introducing
B asking for clarification
C agreeing/disagreeing
D clarifying

b

I'd like to make two points. First, … _____
Can you expand on that? _____
The point is … _____
What's your second point? _____
I was coming to that! _____
Yes, but … _____
I don't agree with that because … _____
Sorry, but who/what are you/we talking about, exactly? _____
We need to be clear here. _____
I'd just like to say that … _____
In what way? _____
Can you give me an example? _____
Look at it this way. _____
What I'm trying to say is, … _____
Absolutely. _____

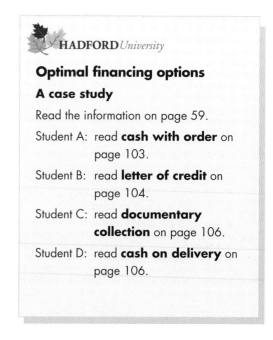

🍁 **HADFORD** *University*

Optimal financing options
A case study

Read the information on page 59.

Student A: read **cash with order** on page 103.

Student B: read **letter of credit** on page 104.

Student C: read **documentary collection** on page 106.

Student D: read **cash on delivery** on page 106.

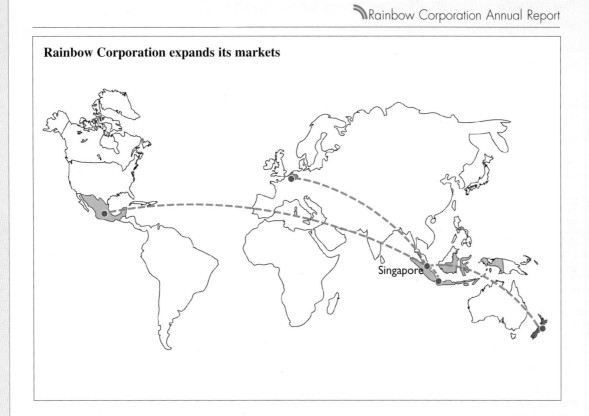

Rainbow Corporation Annual Report

Rainbow Corporation expands its markets

Singapore

Case study

	Indonesia	Belgium	New Zealand	Mexico
Background	Rainbow Corporation in Singapore is an aggressively expanding PC manufacturer. Initially 30% of its products were for the domestic market, with 70% exported to China. In order to double the volume of sales from 20,000 to 40,000 units per annum, the directors have decided to focus on developing further export markets, and the company has now taken orders from Indonesia, Belgium, New Zealand and Mexico. The directors are concerned about the company's ability to finance this growth in business. They have come to the bank to get advice on the optimal payment terms for financing the working capital required (i.e., manufacturing and shipping) for the orders.			
Order	10,000 units private company operating only in Indonesia	2,000 units subsidiary of a large corporation which is an existing client in Singapore	3,000 units New Zealand government	5,000 units private company operating in Mexico only (new client)
Margin	25%	30%	15%	14%
Notes	currently politically unstable very large order = high risk	subsidiary of large corporation; existing client in domestic market = low risk small order with large margin	government order stable economy; good international credit rating = risk free relatively small order	client unknown significant order

Recognizing fixed phrases from banking (1)

There are many fixed phrases in the field of banking.

Examples:

Phrase	Meaning in the discipline
company director	the boss of a company
financial instrument	a document showing acknowledgement of debt
foreign exchange	foreign currencies
exchange rate	the price of one currency against another
capital investment	the money invested in the company

Keep a list of fixed phrases used in banking and remind yourself regularly of the meaning.

Recognizing fixed phrases from academic English (1)

There are also a large number of fixed phrases which are commonly used in academic and technical English in general.

Examples:

Phrase	What comes next?
As we have seen …	a reminder of previous information
An important concept is …	one of the basic points underlying the topic
As you can see, …	a reference to an illustration OR a logical conclusion from previous information
As shown in …	a reference to a diagram or table
… in such a way that …	a result of something
In addition to (X), (Y…)	X = reminder of last point, Y = new point
As well as (X), (Y…)	
In the case of …	a reference to a particular topic or, more often, sub topic
At the same time, …	an action or idea which must be considered alongside another action or idea
… based on …	a piece of research, a theory, an idea
Bear in mind (that) …	key information which helps to explain (or limit in some way) previous information
The point is …	the basic information underlying an explanation
in order to (do X), (Y…)	X = objective, Y = necessary actions/conditions
In financial terms, …	the cost of something previously mentioned
In other words, …	the same information put in a different way
Looking at it another way, …	
In this way …	a result from previous information
Say …	an example
What do I mean by (X)?	an explanation of X

'Given' and 'new' information in sentences

In English, we can put important information at the beginning or at the end of a sentence. There are two types of important information.

1   Information which the listener or reader already knows, from general knowledge or from previous information in the text. This can be called 'given' information. It normally goes at the beginning of the sentence.

2   Information which is new in this text. This can be called 'new' information. It normally goes at the end of a sentence.

Example:
In Lesson 2, the lecturer is talking about financing methods, so financing methods in general = given information.

Given	New
Finance method type 1	*is a letter of credit.*
This method of financing	*involves completing a lot of documentation.*

Introducing new information

We can use special structures to introduce a new topic.

Examples:

Financing methods are my subject today.	➔ ***What I am going to talk about today is** financing methods.*
The size of an order is very important.	➔ ***What is** very **important is** the size of an order.*
Currency fluctuations can cause problems with orders.	➔ ***One reason for problems** with orders **is** currency fluctuations.*
Political or economic instability results in a high risk of payment default.	➔ ***A result of** political or economic instability **is** the risk of payment default.*

Giving sentences a special focus

We sometimes change the normal word order to emphasize a particular point, e.g., a person, an object, a time.

Examples:

Normal sentence	*The Malaysian prime minister placed restrictions on USD payments.*
Focusing on person	*It was the Malaysian prime minister who placed restrictions on …*
Focusing on object	*It was the USD on which the Malaysian prime minister placed restrictions.*
Focusing on time	*It was in the late 1990s that the Malaysian prime minister …*

Clarifying points

When we are speaking, we often have to clarify points. There are many expressions which we can use.

Examples:

Let me put it another way …	*What I'm trying to say is …*
Look at it this way …	*The point/thing is …*

8 OFFSHORE BANKING

synonyms • nouns from verbs • paraphrasing

A Look at the website on the opposite page.

  1 What is meant by *offshore* in banking?

  2 Name some offshore banking locations.

B Look up each noun in box a in a dictionary.

  1 Is it countable, uncountable or both?

  2 What is its banking meaning?

  3 How does it relate to offshore banking?

  4 Make verbs from the nouns if possible.

  5 What useful grammatical information can you find?

C Study the two lists of verbs in box b.

  1 Match the verbs with similar meanings.

  2 Make nouns from the verbs in column 1 if possible.

D Look at the Hadford University handout.

  1 How does the writer restate each section heading in the paragraph?

  2 Find synonyms for the blue words. Use a dictionary if necessary.

  3 Rewrite each sentence to make paraphrases of the texts. Use:

  • synonyms you have found yourself

  • synonyms from Exercise B

  • the nouns you made in Exercise C

  • passives where possible

  • any other words that are necessary

Example:

Early in the 21st century, the International Monetary Fund (IMF) amended the rules for non-resident banking.

→ *The regulations for offshore banking were changed by the IMF (International Monetary Fund) early this century.*

E Study the diagram on the opposite page.

  1 List the boxes in the diagram under the following headings:

   1 Setup procedures

   2 Operating procedures

  2 Write a paragraph entitled *How to set up an offshore bank.*

---

a

| asset | interest | jurisdiction |
| privacy | regulation | stability | tax |

b

1	2
amend	(fully) achieve
contribute (to)	hold
get	keep
maintain	change
maximize	obtain
move	play a role (in)
retain	shift

 **HADFORD** *University*

Concepts in offshore banking

Cross-border capital flows

Low operating costs in other countries can contribute to attracting foreign investors and inflows of foreign money. For example, large corporations may move their capital from one country to another in order to get the best terms and to maximize the investment opportunities in new markets.

Offshore banking regulations

Early in the 21st century, the International Monetary Fund (IMF) amended the rules for non-resident banking. As with onshore banks, offshore banks are required to maintain an international 8% capital-to-asset ratio. That is, banks must retain 8% of their assets as shareholders' capital.

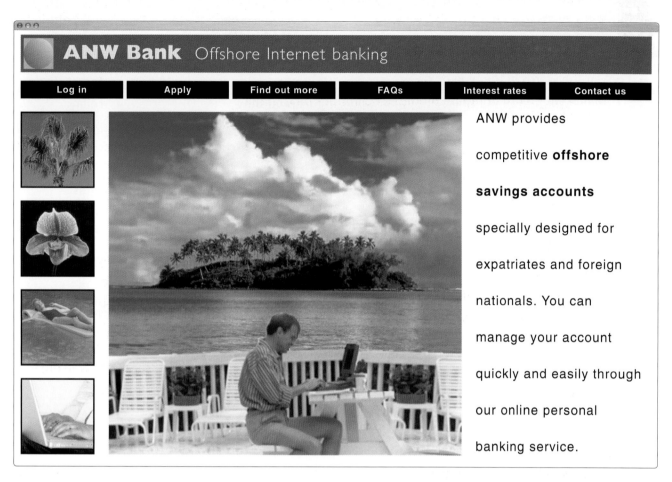

ANW provides competitive **offshore savings accounts** specially designed for expatriates and foreign nationals. You can manage your account quickly and easily through our online personal banking service.

Procedure for setting up an offshore bank

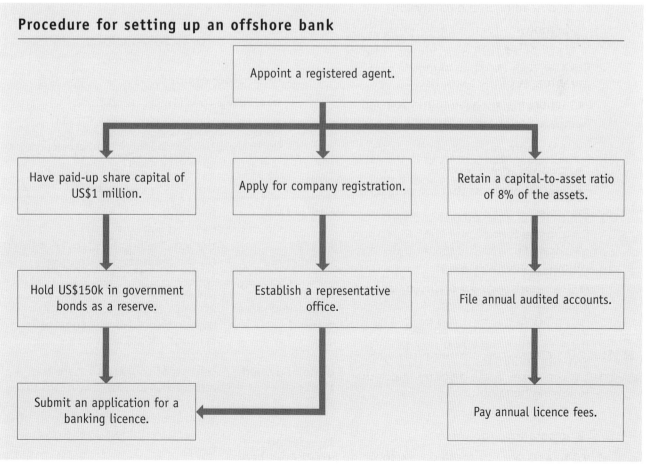

A Look at the words in the blue box.

1 Match each word or phrase on the left with a noun on the right.

2 Make a sentence with each completed expression, showing its banking meaning.

B Look at the four essay types in the Hadford University handout on the right.

1 What should the writer do in each type?

2 Match each essay type with one of the questions (A–D) below the handout.

3 What topics should be covered in each essay question?

C Read the title of the text on the opposite page. Read the first sentence of each paragraph.

1 What will the text be about?

2 Choose one of the essay questions in Exercise B. Write four research questions which will help you to find information for your essay.

D Read the text on the opposite page.

1 Find out whether there is information for your essay question in the text and make notes in your own words. You can also draw on your own knowledge.

2 Work with another person who has chosen the same essay question as you. Compare your notes.

E Study the highlighted sentences in the text.

1 Underline all the subjects and their verbs.

2 Which is the main subject and verb for each sentence?

F Study the table on the right.

1 Match each word or phrase with its meaning.

2 Underline the words or phrases in the text which the writer uses to give the definitions.

asset	fees
capital flow	ceiling
financial	procedures
financial disclosure	controls
interest rate	product
licensing and administration	rates
tax	protection

HADFORD *University*

There are four main essay types in banking studies:

• descriptive

• analytical

• comparison

• argument

(A) What are the advantages and disadvantages for banks of establishing offshore facilities?

(B) What questions do offshore banks need to ask to ensure their clients do not have criminal or terrorist associations? Describe some client screening procedures they could implement.

(C) Explain why the term 'tax haven' could be considered misleading.

(D) 'Offshore banks have an important role to play in the financial services industry.' To what extent do you agree with this statement?

Word/phrase	Meaning
1 low tax jurisdictions	the legal selling of shares not listed on the main stock exchange
2 over-the-counter trading	the process whereby criminals attempt to conceal the origin and ownership of funds generated through illegal activities
3 parallel-owned banks	centres or countries where the authorities impose low or no taxes
4 money laundering	separate legal entities but with the same shareholders as the onshore bank

Offshore banking – why, what and where?

It was during the 1960s and 1970s that offshore financial centres were first set up. Operating outside the depositors' country of residence, these facilities offered offshore banking and new interbank markets with significant financial and legal advantages. In addition to low or no taxation, offshore banks in these centres met the demand for client banking privacy and anonymity, a less restrictive legal framework and easy access to deposits. The impetus for their emergence was the imposition, in industrial countries, of a range of restrictive financial regulations. These included the introduction of interest rate ceilings, bank reserve requirements, restrictions on the range of financial products, capital flow controls, new procedures for financial disclosure, an increase in tax rates and the expansion of taxable transactions.

The term 'offshore' refers to a situation where all banking and financial transactions are conducted in a foreign currency and are carried out by non-residents. Offshore banks operate in low tax jurisdictions – centres or countries where taxes have been kept low in order to encourage non-resident businesses to locate there. Hence they have become known as 'tax havens'. Most offshore banks are located in small island nations, for example the Channel Islands, the Cayman Islands, the Isle of Man and the Bahamas, although they also include landlocked jurisdictions such as Switzerland, Luxembourg, and Andorra. For many of these countries, a key objective was to generate income through licensing and administration fees and related support services revenue.

The structure of offshore banks often differs from that of onshore banks. They may be a related legal entity, or a branch of an onshore bank with a limited physical presence, such as 'shell' branches of an onshore bank. Some are parallel-owned banks, that is, they are not subsidiaries but may share common ownership or have interlinked businesses with a defined banking group.

Offshore banks may offer any or all of the onshore banking services. They may also offer other services such as over-the-counter trading (for example, in derivatives), which is trading in shares not listed on the main or official stock exchange. Because they operate with a lower cost base than onshore banks, some have been able to offer higher interest rates. Asset protection is another motivation for banking offshore. It can also be a safer option for individuals residing in locations where there is political and/or economic instability and corruption.

A common misconception is that offshore banking is associated with dubious activities such as tax evasion, terrorism and money laundering (the process through which criminal gangs try to conceal the origins of their money), and that therefore it is illegal. This is not the case. However, in order to protect themselves from undesirable clients, offshore banks should have a robust screening process. Questions which need to be considered by offshore banks in relation to potential clients include their identity, their financial standing, the nature of their business, and the source of their funds.

Another misconception is that offshore account holders are not required to make a declaration of income earned offshore and that consequently there is a significant tax advantage for offshore bank customers. This perception arises because, unlike onshore banks, there is no legal requirement for offshore banks to report customer account information to other tax authorities. However, in many countries there are laws or regulations in place that allow for interest earned on bank accounts to be tax-free – either for their own citizens, foreigners only, or maybe both. There is no distinction made between interest earned on income onshore or offshore. The non-declaration of income or tax evasion on offshore income is illegal in most countries and the responsibility to declare it lies with the account holder, not the bank.

In theory, an offshore banking facility can be established by any individual or group that can pay the setup, licensing and administration fees. But the reality in the 21st century is that it is mainly multinational corporations and onshore banks that create offshore banking facilities.

A Find the words in the box in the text in Lesson 2.

  1 What part of speech is each word?

  2 Think of another word which could be used in place of the word in the text. Use your dictionary if necessary.

> depositor   impetus   imposition
> restriction   disclosure   expansion
> generate   interlinked   standing
> perception

B Study sentences A–D on the right.

  1 Identify the dependent clause.

  2 Copy the table under the sentences and write the parts of each dependent clause in the table.

  3 Rewrite the sentence using an active construction.

  Example:

  Here is a list of questions which offshore banks have to consider.

(A) Here is a list of questions which have to be considered by offshore banks.

(B) They operate in countries where taxes have been kept low.

(C) The term 'offshore' refers to a situation in which all banking and financial transactions are carried out by non-residents.

(D) However, it is clear that questions are now being asked by the tax authorities.

C Look at the essay plans and extracts on the opposite page.

  1 Match each plan with an essay question in Lesson 2.

  2 Which essay is each extract from?

  3 Which part of the plan is each extract from?

Subject	Verb	By whom/what
(questions) which	have to be considered	by offshore banks

D Work with a partner.

  1 Write another paragraph for one of the plans.

  2 Exchange paragraphs with another pair. Can they identify where it comes from?

A Make complete sentences from these notes. Add words as necessary.

(A) offshore facilities – located – foreign jurisdictions – less regulation + taxation

(B) several key advantages – banks – providing offshore facilities

(C) offshore banking services – provided by many banks – customers wanting privacy/anonymyity/good return on investment

(D) however, banks face dilemma – fiscal transparency/maintaining client privacy

(E) advantages outweigh disadvantages – provided effective controls

(F) also, future risk – if favourable tax legislation introduced – onshore banks make offshore less attractive

B The sentences in Exercise A are topic sentences for paragraphs from essay A in Lesson 2. Put them in the best order for the essay. What is the main topic for each paragraph?

C Look at the essay question on the right.

  1 What kind of essay is this?

  2 Do some research and make a plan.

  3 Write the essay.

Richard Allen, an American resident, invested US$1 million in an offshore bank located in Taluva, a Pacific Island, in a hedge fund that was not permitted to operate onshore in the US. Within a year, as a result of a political upheaval and change of government in Taluva, the offshore bank's licence was cancelled and the bank closed. The remote location of Taluva caused Mr Allen difficulties in tracing and establishing title to his investment. In addition, he had not realized that the administration fees were so great. The result was a substantially lower net return than advertised. What conclusions would you draw from Mr Allen's experience?

Essay plans

A

1 Introduction: definition + importance of client screening for offshore banks

2 Types of undesirable activities clients may be involved in

3 Recommended screening procedures, e.g., KYC (proof of identity, proof of address, source of funds, etc.); cooperating with law-enforcement agencies; policies, staff training

4 Difficulties with implementing screening procedures

5 Conclusion: screening procedures should be effective provided the 'right' questions are asked

B

1 Introduction: financial services industry; give essay aims

2 Definition of offshore banking

3 The role of offshore banking; how it complements other financial services

4 Any reasons to disagree with the statement

5 Conclusion: agree with the statement

Essay extracts

1

Offshore banking is one sector within the broader financial services industry, which encompasses a variety of services related to money and investment including banks, credit card companies, insurance companies, stock and share brokers and other organizations that deal with the management of money. This essay will discuss the role of offshore banking within the financial services industry. Firstly, the term offshore banking will be defined, and key differences between offshore and onshore banking established.

Offshore banking refers to banking services which are provided for non-residents and which are carried out in a foreign currency. Offshore banks may offer any or all of the services offered by onshore banks. However, they may also include other services such as over-the-counter trading, and provide higher interest rates than onshore banks.

2

A common perception of offshore banking is that it is a clandestine activity associated with organized crime, terrorist groups, and dubious practices such as money laundering and tax evasion. In the aftermath of September 11, 2001, and the perception that some offshore banks were repositories for the terrorists' funds, there has been increased pressure on offshore banks to review their client screening procedures. This pressure has come from countries such as the US, international bodies such as the Financial Action Task Force (FATF) and from the international monetary authorities.

In December 1988 the Basel Committee on Banking Supervision issued a list of principles and procedures designed to prevent criminal use of the banking system. It focused on all aspects of money laundering through the banking system, including concealment of money obtained by illicit means, such as drug trafficking, robbery, terrorism and fraud. Some of the recommended procedures included 'know your client' (KYC) guidelines. These stipulated that banks should obtain proof of the client's identity, proof of their address, the source of their funds, etc. In addition, they recommended that offshore banks should cooperate fully with national law-enforcement agencies (within the constraints of the customer confidentiality rules), and that the banks should incorporate policies and staff training supporting the recommended principles.

Understanding new words: using definitions

You will often find new words in academic texts. Sometimes you will not be able to understand the text unless you look the word up in a dictionary, but often a technical term will be defined or explained immediately or later in the text.

Look for these indicators:

is or *are*	*The term 'tax haven'* **is** *basically about …*
brackets	*… money laundering* **(***the process through which criminal gangs try to conceal the origins of their money***)***.*
or	*However, the non-declaration of income,* **or** *tax evasion, on offshore income, …*
which	*… over the counter trading,* **which is** *trading in shares not listed on the main or official stock exchange.*
a comma or a dash (–) immediately after the word or phrase	*… low tax jurisdictions – centres or countries where taxes have been kept low …*
phrases such as *in other words, that is*	*… some are parallel-owned banks:* **that is***, they are not subsidiaries but may share common ownership …*

Remember!

When you write assignments, you may want to define words yourself. Learn to use the methods above to give variety to your written work.

Understanding direction verbs in essay titles

Special verbs called **direction verbs** are used in essay titles. Each direction verb indicates a type of essay. You must understand the meaning of these words so you can choose the correct writing plan.

Kind of essay	Direction verbs
Descriptive	*State … Say … Outline … Describe … Summarize … What is/are …?*
Analytical	*Analyse … Explain … Comment on … Examine … Give reasons for … Why …? How …?*
Comparison/ evaluation	*Compare (and contrast) … Distinguish between … Evaluate … What are the advantages and/or disadvantages of …?*
Argument	*Discuss … Consider … (Critically) evaluate … To what extent …? How far …?*

Choosing the correct writing plan

When you are given a written assignment, you must decide on the best writing plan before you begin to write the outline. Use key words in the essay title to help you choose – see *Vocabulary bank*.

Type of essay – content	Possible structure
Descriptive writing List **the most important points** of something: e.g., in a narrative, a list of key events in chronological order; a description of key ideas in a theory or from an article you have read. Summarize points in a logical order. **Example**: *What questions do offshore banks need to ask to ensure their clients do not have criminal associations?*	• **introduction** • **point/event 1** • **point/event 2** • **point/event 3** • **conclusion**
Analytical writing List the **important points** which **in your opinion** explain the situation. Justify your opinion in each case. Look behind the facts at the **how** and **why**, not just **what/who/when**. Look for and question accepted ideas and assumptions. **Example**: *Explain why the term 'tax haven' could be considered misleading.*	• **introduction** • **definitions** • **most important point:** example/evidence/reason 1 example/evidence/reason 2 etc. • **next point:** example/evidence/reason 3 example/evidence/reason 4 etc. • **conclusion**
Comparison/evaluation Decide on and define the **aspects** to compare two subjects. You may use these aspects as the basis for paragraphing. Evaluate which aspect(s) is/are better or preferable and give reasons/criteria for your judgment. **Example**: *What are the advantages and disadvantages for banks of establishing offshore facilities?*	• **introduction** • **state and define aspects** *Either*: • **aspect 1:** subject A v. B • **aspect 2:** subject A v. B *Or*: • **subject A:** aspect 1, 2, etc. • **subject B:** aspect 1, 2, etc. etc. • **conclusion/evaluation**
Argument writing **Analyse** and/or **evaluate**, then give your **opinion** in a **thesis statement** at the beginning or the end. Show awareness of difficulties and disagreements by mentioning counter-arguments. **Support** your opinion with evidence. **Example**: *'Offshore banks have an important role to play in the financial services industry.' To what extent do you agree with this statement?*	• **introduction: statement of issue** • **thesis statement giving opinion** • **define terms** • **point 1:** explain + evidence • **point 2:** explain + evidence etc. • **conclusion:** implications, etc. *Alternatively*: • **introduction: statement of issue** • **define terms** • **for:** point 1, 2, etc. • **against:** point 1, 2, etc. • **conclusion: statement of opinion**

BANKING IN DEVELOPING COUNTRIES

9.1 Vocabulary   fixed phrases

A   Match the words to make fixed phrases.

1	economic	based
2	financial	capita
3	income	country
4	industrialized	free
5	interest	indicators
6	nationalized	industry
7	per	liberalization

	1	**2**
	in	on ... one hand
		... most cases
	most	... start with
	some	to ... extent
		on ... other hand
	the	on ... grounds that
	to	... people think

B   Study the words and phrases in the blue box.

   1   Complete each phrase in column 2 with a word from column 1.

   2   Which phrase can you use to:

- begin talking about several points?
- talk about certain circumstances?
- compare two ideas?
- mention an idea?
- agree only partially with a point?
- give a reason for a point?

C   Read the extract from the Hadford University handout about developing nations and banking on this page.

   1   Match the blue words in this extract with the definitions on the opposite page.

   2   Use your dictionary to check words you do not know.

D   Look at the pictures on the opposite page. What does each picture show? How do they relate to developed and developing countries?

E   Read sentences A–F on the opposite page. Replace the words in italics with a phrase from Exercise B.

F   Complete the table on the right.

   1   Mark the nouns in the first column as countable (C), uncountable (U) or both.

   2   Find other related forms of the word and mark their part of speech.

HADFORD *University*

How can we divide countries into 'developed' and 'developing'? There is no standard basis but the following points are worth noting.

- The World Bank and IMF focus on income and economic indicators for assessing a country's development status.
- The economies of developed countries tend to have a high GDP and a high degree of financial liberalization.
- In a less developed country the per capita income is very low and the infrastructure poor.
- In many less developed countries with low-income economies, bank mergers, acquisitions and liquidations occurred during the late 1990s.
- In developing countries, from 1999 onwards the number of nationalized commercial banks declined due to restructuring.
- In the decade to 2004 privatization and foreign ownership of banks increased in these countries.

Word		Other related forms	
credit	(n C/U)	creditor	
economy			
expense			
finance			
industrial			
invest			
national			
privatize			
profit			
region			
trade			

A The term 'developed country' *usually* refers to its economic development.

B The term 'low-income economy' has several meanings. *Firstly*, it refers to an economy based on agriculture and natural resource extraction.

C The terms 'less developed countries' and 'low-income economies' *partially* refer to countries with low wages and unskilled labour.

D The term 'newly industrialized country' (NIC) is an economic category and is not based on income. *However*, countries with lower to middle incomes dominate.

E The term 'emerging market' crosses all the World Bank income classifications, except high-income economies; but it refers mainly to low-income economies *because* it is per capita based.

F It is *generally believed* that the OECD member countries and other high-income economies represent the developed countries.

Hadford University.ac.uk/bank/

www.hadford.ac.uk/bank/def · Google

HADFORDUniversity | Home | Archive | Departments | News | Help

Definitions

A a part of the United Nations which encourages international trade and gives financial help to poor countries

B belonging to a company from another country

C an international organization which was formed in 1945 to help economic development, especially of poorer countries

D closing a company and selling its assets, often because it is unable to pay its debts

E money earned

F selling a nationalized industry to private owners

G the amount of income for each individual person

H the basic systems and services, such as transport and power supplies, that a country or organization uses in order to work effectively

I when two or more companies join together

J when a company buys an asset, e.g., another company, a building, etc.

K the total value of goods and services produced by a country in a year

L government owned and operated; not controlled by private owners

M making laws or systems relating to money less strict

N various statistics (e.g., unemployment rate) indicating short-term and long-term economic performance

O organizing a company in a new way to make it operate more efficiently

A Study the slide on the right.

1 Make a list of questions that you expect the lecturer to answer.

2 Read the notes and the review questions in the student notes below. What information is missing?

B 🎧 Listen to Part 1 of the lecture.

1 Complete the *Notes* section below.

2 Complete the *Summary* section.

3 Answer the *Review* questions.

C 🎧 Study the phrases in column 1 of the blue box. Listen to some sentences from the lecture. Which type of information in column 2 follows each phrase?

D 🎧 Create a blank Cornell diagram. Listen to Part 2 of the lecture.

1 Complete the *Notes* section.

2 Complete the *Review* and *Summary* sections.

3 Were your questions in Exercise A answered?

 HADFORD *University*

Banking in developing countries (Lecture 1)

● Defining the types of economies

● Types of banking institution
  ■ for economic development
  ■ for commercial banking

1	2
1 It could be argued that …	information about a point the speaker will make later
2 As we shall see …	
3 From the point of view of …	a statement the speaker agrees with
	a conclusion
4 It's true to say that …	an idea the speaker may or may not agree with
5 So it should be clear that …	

Review

Main distinction between developing and other countries?
Definitions depend on …

'Developed' countries are …
World Bank categories?
(5 income-based).

Low-income economies also called …

_____

NICs are …?
Developing countries as % world?

Banking institutions
(What do they provide?)
3 major multilateral groups
are …

Their focus is …
4th category focuses on …?

Summary

Notes

Terms and definitions: 'developing' v. other countries
No definitive classification; depends on who and why, e.g.,
 ● _____ – development indicators
 ● investors and market index makers – level of '_____
So-called 'developed' = _____ members = high-income
World Bank 5 income-based categories:
 1) high OECD   2) high   3) upper middle
 4) lower middle   5) low
_____ income economies ≈
 ■ LDCs or _____ countries
 ■ HIPCs or _____
 ■ poor infrastructure; based on _____ and _____

Lower-middle-income economies ≈ NICs or _____
'Developing' countries ≈ _____ % of the world's countries

Types of banking institution
 ● daily business – _____ banks
 ● economic development - _____ banks (3 types):
  1) MDBs or multilateral _____ banks (large regional)
  2) MFIs or multilateral _____ institutions (smaller, more specific)
  3) Sub- _____ banks
Multilateral banks - _____ programmes
4th category = … _____ institutions

9.3 Extending skills

recognizing digressions • source references

A Study the words and phrases in box a.

1 Mark the stressed syllables.

2 🎧 Listen and check your answers.

3 Which is the odd one out in each group? Why?

B Study the phrases in box b.

1 Do the phrases show a digression (start or end) or a relevant point? Write **D** or **R**.

2 Look at the **D** phrases. Do they start or end the digression?

C 🎧 Listen to the final part of the lecture from Lesson 2.

1 Take notes using the Cornell system. Leave spaces if you miss information.

2 What topic does the lecturer mention that is different from the main subject?

3 Why does he mention this topic?

4 What is your research task?

5 Compare your notes in pairs. Fill in any blank spaces.

6 Complete the *Review* and *Summary* sections.

a
1 infrastructure, nationalized, financial, merger
2 income based, banking structures, member countries, developing region
3 markets, regions, economies, countries
4 international institutions, multilateral banks, emerging markets, competitive terms

b
It's the first of these points that I'm going to focus on now …

Now where was I?

By the way, …

So to get back to the main topic …

If we can move on now to …

You don't need to take notes on this …

If we turn now to …

D 🎧 What information does the lecturer provide about sources? Listen to the extracts and complete the table below.

	Extract 1	Extract 2	Extract 3	Extract 4
Name of writer				
Title and date of source				
Location				
Type of reference				
Relevant to …?				
Introducing phrase				

E Use your notes to write 75–100 words about foreign direct investment.

F Work in groups. Study the three types of commercial bank ownership in developing countries (see box c). Choose one type and then discuss these questions.

1 What kind of information will you need to find?

2 What ideas do you already have?

3 Where can you go to find more information?

c
private domestic commercial banks
foreign-owned commercial banks
state-owned commercial banks

A Look up the words in the blue box. Identify their stress patterns.

accountability   economic   enterprise
evasion   nationalization   private
privatization   requirements   reserves

B Work in pairs.

Student A: Think of good ways to take part in a seminar.

Student B: Think of bad ways to take part in a seminar.

Table 1

	✓/✗	Reasons
Extract 1		
Extract 2		
Extract 3		
Extract 4		

C You are going to hear some students in a seminar. They have been asked to discuss the question: 'What problems do banks in developing countries face?'

  1 🎧 Listen to the seminar extracts and complete Table 1. Put a ✓ for a good contribution and a ✗ for a poor one.

  2 Give reasons for your opinion.

  3 Identify some additional information in the good contributions.

HADFORD*University*

Faculty of Banking

Seminar Topic 1

Prepare a presentation on the following topic:

Analyse and comment on the data presented in Graph 1, specifying reasons for the trends relating to foreign-owned banks.

D Study Graph 1 on the opposite page. In pairs or groups, discuss the following questions.

  1 What does the information show about commercial bank ownership?

  2 What other information not given here might be useful in explaining the trends shown in the graph?

E Study the seminar topic in the Hadford University handout. Work in a group of three or four.

  1 Make notes on the seminar topic.

  2 Discuss your information for the topics in Lesson 3, Exercise F. Agree on the best definition of the type of bank you have chosen.

  3 Discuss how best to include this information in the seminar topic.

  4 Prepare your presentation, including a definition and description of your topic, and notes from the lectures.

  5 Give your presentation to the whole class.

F Study Table 2 on the opposite page. In pairs, discuss the following questions.

  1 What does Table 2 show?

  2 What do you think is the most significant information? Present a brief explanation to your partner.

Pudong, the financial district of Shanghai, China

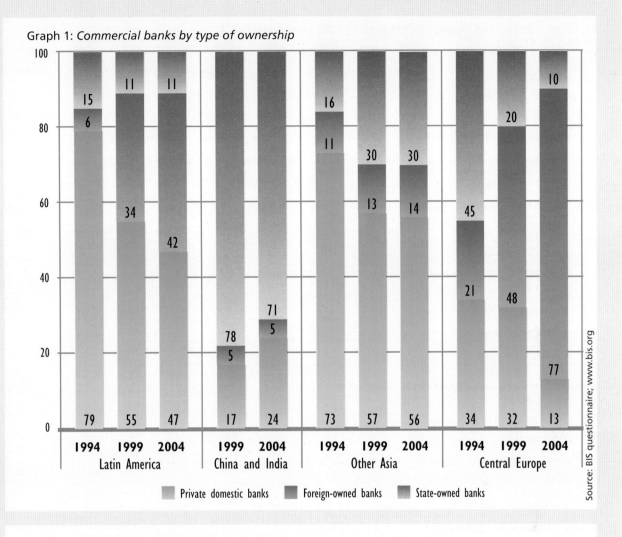

Graph 1: *Commercial banks by type of ownership*

Source: BIS questionnaire; www.bis.org

Private domestic banks   Foreign-owned banks   State-owned banks

Table 2: *Source of foreign bank assets, by region*
Percentage of foreign bank assets in host region owned by banks from other regions

		Source region						
		East Asia & Pacific	Europe & Central Asia	Latin America & Caribbean	Middle East & Northern Africa	South Asia	Sub-Saharan Africa	High-income economies
Host Region	East Asia & Pacific	6.39						93.61
	Europe & Central Asia		1.84		0.01			98.15
	Latin America & Caribbean			4.78				95.22
	Middle East & Northern Africa				8.91			91.09
	South Asia					0.74	19.51	79.75
	Sub-Saharan Africa	0.07	0.03	0.02	0.29	1.99	14.12	83.48

Source: http://papers.ssrn.com/sol3/papers.cfm?abastract_id=904659

Notes: A foreign bank is defined to have at least 50 per cent foreign ownership. Foreign assets are averages over the 2000–2004 period. Region classifications follow World Bank definitions as published in *Global Development Finance* (2006).

Recognizing fixed phrases from banking (2)

Make sure you understand these phrases from banking.

domestic bank	*less developed country (LDC)*
economic indicator	*multilateral development bank (MDB)*
emerging market	*multilateral financial institution (MFI)*
financial liberalization	*nationalized industry*
foreign direct investment (FDI)	*newly industrialized country (NIC)*
foreign ownership	*per capita income*
highly indebted poor country (HIPC)	*source country*
host country	*state-owned bank*

Recognizing fixed phrases from academic English (2)

Make sure you understand these fixed phrases from general spoken academic English.

As we shall see, …	*Most people think …*
Bearing in mind that …	*On the grounds that …*
But the real question is …	*On the one hand, …*
From the point of view of …	*On the other hand, …*
If we turn now to …	*Research has shown that …*
In most cases …	*So it should be clear that …*
In the sense that …	*So to get back to the main topic …*
That's the reason why …	*To some extent …*
It could be argued that …	*To start with, …*
It's true to say that …	

Using the Cornell note-taking system

There are many ways to take notes from a lecture. One method was developed by Walter Pauk at Cornell University, USA.

The system involves **Five Rs**.

record	Take notes during the lecture.
reduce	After the lecture, turn the notes into one- or two-word questions or 'cues' which will help you remember the key information.
recite	Say the questions and answers aloud.
reflect	Decide on the best way to summarize the key information in the lecture.
review	Look again at the key words and the summary (and do this regularly).

Recognizing digressions

Lecturers sometimes move away from the main point in a lecture to tell a story or an anecdote. This is called a **digression**. You must be able to recognize the start and end of digressions in a lecture.

Sometimes a digression is directly relevant to the content of the lecture, sometimes it has some relevance and sometimes, with a poor lecturer, it may be completely irrelevant. Sometimes the lecturer points out the relevance.

Don't worry if you get lost in a digression. Just leave a space in your notes and ask people afterwards.

Recognizing the start	That reminds me …
	I remember once …
	By the way …
Recognizing the end	Anyway, where was I?
	Back to the point.
	So, as I was saying …

Understanding the relevance	Of course, the point of that story is …
	I'm sure you can all see that the story shows …
	Why did I tell that story? Well, …

Asking about digressions	What was the point about the Cornell note-taking system?
	Why did he start talking about note-taking?
	I didn't get the bit about …

Referring to other people's ideas

We often need to talk about the ideas of other people in a lecture or a tutorial. We normally give the name of the writer, and/or the name of the source. We usually introduce the reference with a phrase; we may quote directly, or we may paraphrase an idea.

Name and introducing phrase	As Heffernan points out …
	To quote Heffernan …
Where	in Modern Banking …
What	the foreign firm can bring in expertise …

A Study the words in box a.

  1 Use your dictionary to find out the meanings.

  2 What part of speech is each word?

> **a**
> activity   borrow   customer
> energy   enterprise   ethics   fund
> impact   industry   lend   trade

B Read the Hadford University handout.

  1 Use your dictionary or another source to check the meanings of the highlighted phrases.

  2 Which are the stressed syllables in each phrase?

C Look at the pictures on the opposite page.

  1 What ethical issue does each picture depict?

  2 For each picture, write a sentence about the role of ethical banks. Use highlighted phrases from Exercise B and words from Exercise A.

D Study the words in box b.

  1 Check the meanings, parts of speech and stress patterns.

  2 Put the words into the correct box in the table below, as in the example.

Neutral	Marked
rise, increase	rocket, soar
fall, decrease	
big, large	
good	
small	

HADFORD *University*

Ethical banks

An increasing number of banks have a well-publicized ethical stance, offering their clients socially responsible investments in, for example, alternative energy projects, such as wind or solar power. Ethical banks provide the standard financial and banking services but with a focus on social gain, as opposed to financial gain. Customers evaluate ethical banks on a range of issues, from whether they finance companies involved in the tobacco industry, or terrorist activities, to their stance on environmental issues, such as deforestation and greenhouse gas emissions. Policy areas covered by the ethical online bank Smile include human rights, the arms trade, genetic modification, ecological impact, animal welfare, social enterprise, corporate responsibility and global trade.

> **b**
> brilliant   collapse   enormous   huge
> insignificant   massive   minimal   outstanding
> plummet   plunge   rocket   significant   slump
> soar   superb   tremendous

E Read the extract from the Very Ethical Bank chairman's letter to customers.

  1 Use a marked word in place of each of the blue (neutral) words.

  2 Look at the red phrases. How strong or confident are they?

It's clear that, since we launched our ethical policy, customer support has risen. There are undoubtedly types of business activity our customers do not want us to support; and it's generally accepted that we have a good set of ethical principles guiding our investments, as every three years we obtain a new mandate from our customers.

It's fair to say that, for some of our policies, the impact is not always large or immediately apparent.

But, because all new business proposals are assessed against our ethical policy, regardless of potential financial gain, you can be confident that we will not let our ethical standards fall.

It is unlikely that we would refuse banking services to large industries if there was no apparent conflict with our ethical policy. However, before we reach a decision, there may be a need for further research in a small number of cases.

A Study the sentence on the right.
Each phrase in box a could go in the space. What effect would each one have on the base meaning? Mark from *** = very confident to * = very tentative.

B Survey the text on the opposite page.
  1 What will the text be about?
  2 Write three research questions.

C Read the text. Does it answer your questions?

D Answer these questions.
  1 What does the word 'green' mean when used to describe investments?
  2 How did the interest in SRIs begin?
  3 Why might an ethical bank decide not to lend money to a particular client?
  4 What evidence does the writer give that ethical investment is a significant part of banking activity?
  5 Has the implementation of the Equator Principles been a success?

E Find the phrases in box b in the text.
Is the writer *confident* (C) or *tentative* (T) about the information which follows?

F Look at the writer's description of the Equator Principles initiative (paragraph 5).
  1 Underline the marked words.
  2 What does the choice of these words tell you about the writer's opinion of the Principles?
  3 Find neutral words to use in their place.

G Study the example sentence on the right, and then sentences A and B.
  1 Divide sentences A and B into small parts, as in the example sentence.
  2 Underline any joining words (e.g., conjunctions).
  3 Find the subjects, verbs, objects/complements and adverbial phrases which go together.
  4 Make several short simple sentences which show the meaning.

High-profile charity and media campaigns
_____
the increase of client interest in socially responsible investing.

a
probably caused _____
may have contributed to _____
were possibly one of the factors which contributed to _____
could have been a factor which led to _____
caused _____
seem to have caused _____

b
It is obvious … _____
Many writers seem to agree … _____
It appears to be the case … _____
many writers have claimed … _____
the evidence does not support … _____
a recent survey has found … _____
much of the data suggests … _____

Example:

Generally | deposit *customers* | have not questioned | *banks* | on their lending policies, | provided | *they* | are receiving | good *returns* on their investments.

A

Other investors may exclude companies from their investment pool because they 'engage in business practices that are viewed by investor groups as socially harmful or morally–ethically repugnant'.

B

In June 2003, ten international commercial banks adopted the World Bank International Finance Corporation's strict but 'voluntary set of guidelines for managing environmental and social issues in project finance lending'.

Socially responsible investments and the Equator Principles

Banking is regulated in most countries. Regulatory authorities grant banks authorization to trade and provide banking services. For traditional banks, the main purpose is to maximize profits for their shareholders from transaction fees on their services, and interest charged on loans. For borrowers who meet their lending criteria, they provide financial products at reasonable rates. For deposit customers, they provide good returns, in terms of interest on secure investments or deposits, while operating within national banking laws. The bank's investment focus is mainly on short-term financial instruments, usually with a maximum term of five years. Generally, deposit customers have not questioned banks on their lending policies, provided they are receiving good returns on their investments. However, in recent years, more and more borrowers have become concerned about who money is lent to and for what purposes.

Many writers have claimed that massive media interest in social and green issues has raised public awareness of the 'price' attached to the environmental impact of business: deforestation, unsustainable development, carbon and greenhouse gas emissions, for example. There has been a corresponding increase in consumer-led demand for investments in socially responsible companies. It appears to be the case that environmental activists have changed their focus from the large corporations involved in unsustainable industries (e.g., logging or mining) and human rights abuse (e.g., sweatshop labour or abuse of the rights of indigenous peoples), to publicly confronting the large banking corporations that finance them. Some of these corporations have responded by offering socially responsible investments (SRIs) to investors 'seeking with their investment dollars to support corporations that have a beneficial impact on society'(Smith et al, 2003, p. 100).

Many writers seem to agree that the definition of SRI is problematic. It is obvious that what constitutes a socially responsible investment is not the same for everyone. As Sethi (2005) states, some 'investors screen companies for socio-economic and environmental goals having first met their financial goals' (p. 101). Other investors may exclude companies from their investment pool because of their core business (e.g., tobacco), or because they 'engage in business practices that are viewed by investor groups as socially harmful or morally–ethically repugnant' (Sethi, op.cit., p.101–2).

A recent survey has found that, between 2003 and 2004, 'broad' SRI resulted in significant growth for the European ethical wealth management market and that 'core SRI in the UK is worth €30.5 billion, while the broad SRI market is worth €781 billion' (Langridge, 2006). In June 2003, ten international commercial banks adopted the World Bank International Finance Corporation's strict but 'voluntary set of guidelines for managing environmental and social issues in project finance lending' (www.ifc.org/equatorprinciples). As signatories, these banks or Equator Principles Financial Institutions (EPFIs) agree to conform to the ten principles, named the 'Equator Principles', which set international environmental and social-impact standards for financing projects with capital costs of US$10 million or more.

The impact of the Equator Principles has been impossible to assess, due in part to the lack of transparency. However, much of the data suggests that the critical problem is enforcing compliance. As a result, in June 2006 the Principles were revised and the level of scrutiny of EPFIs was upgraded. This has not been enough, however, to satisfy BankTrack who, along with other non-government organizations monitoring private bank lending practices, have continued to attack the implementation. They criticize the financing of new projects (such as dam construction, or oil and gas exploration) on the grounds of their disastrous social impacts (Vogel, 2006). But according to Vogel (op.cit.), the evidence does not support their views, since many of these projects 'make outstanding contributions to local and national development'.

While the Equator Principles signatories are large international banks, the high street banks are also involved in endorsing and promoting socially responsible banking options. For example, some provide options in the form of charity credit cards where issuers and users contribute a percentage of the takings to international charities. Some banks have differentiated themselves as 'ethical banks', focusing on positive investment in certain areas, or emphasizing the exclusion of others, such as the sale or manufacture of armaments. Smile (a branch of the ethical Co-operative Bank) operates exclusively online. Online banking is promoted as having large paper-saving and identity-theft prevention benefits as well.

A Read the four essay questions on the right. What types of essay are they?

B Look at text A on the opposite page. Copy and complete Table 1 below.

C Look at text B on the opposite page. Copy and complete Table 2 below.

D Read the title of Essay 4 again.

    1 Make a plan for this essay.

    2 Write a topic sentence for each paragraph in the body of the essay.

    3 Write a concluding paragraph.

1 Outline the problems and solutions in obtaining bank finance for a business involved in alternative energy.

2 Explain, from a bank's viewpoint, the dilemma it faces in providing socially responsible investments for customers.

3 Consider a bank that provides finance for sustainable development projects. What questions might the bank ask a business applying for project finance?

4 A company is planning to develop a waste recycling business. It wants to obtain finance from a bank supporting socially responsible investments. Explain the business plan and discuss the risks, benefits and finance needs of the project.

Table 1

Situation	
Problems	
Solutions	

Table 2

Solution	
Argument in favour	
Argument against	

A Expand these simple sentences. Add extra information. Use the ideas in Lesson 3.

    1 The proposal is for waste recycling.

    2 The practice of dumping waste in a landfill will create a long-term environmental risk.

    3 A risk to the project is competition from other entrants to the market.

    4 The business plan is sound.

    5 This is a long-term business plan.

B Look at text C on the opposite page. Copy and complete Tables 1–3.

C Look at text D on the opposite page.

    1 Complete a further row of Table 1.

    2 How could you write this as a reference?

D What do the abbreviations in the blue box mean?

Table 1: *Referencing books*

Author(s)	Publisher	Date	Place

Table 2: *Referencing journals*

Name of journal	Volume	Pages

Table 3: *Referencing websites*

Retrieval date	URL

&	©	cf.	edn.	ed(s).	et al.
ibid.	n.d.	op. cit.	p.	pp.	vol.

E Look again at the text in Lesson 2 and text B on the opposite page.

    1 Find all the direct quotations and their source references.

    2 What words are used to introduce each direct quote? Why does the writer choose each word?

    3 What punctuation is used to introduce each direct quote?

F Write out a reference list for your essay in Lesson 3, Exercise D.

Case Study 1

In 2000, John Goodman decided to start a small business specializing in sustainable energy, namely developing and manufacturing solar panels for home owners. John prepared a business plan to show that, while initially expensive to install, over time his solar power panels would be energy- and cost-efficient, provided they were correctly installed.

He applied to his bank for a ten-year loan for fixed capital costs, and a three-year loan for working capital. His high street bank refused him a loan on the grounds that his business idea was 'too exotic', and argued that, as the market was a niche not mainstream market, it was too small to provide even reasonable returns. It also argued that governments were more interested in nuclear and biofuels as an alternative, as solar power was not yet proven to be cost effective. Furthermore, like most traditional banks, its focus was mainly on short-term financial instruments.

Following his bank's refusal to loan him the finance, John searched the Internet for banks offering funding for sustainable energy projects. After selecting three possible banks as sources of finance for his project, he re-read their lending criteria and refined his technology and business plans before submitting his application to a retail bank selling itself as an 'ethical bank'. On its Internet site, the 'ethical bank' stated that it refused to lend or invest in companies with poor environmental records. This time John was successful in his loan application. And unlike traditional banks, the 'ethical bank' was prepared to grant John both a ten-year loan and a three-year loan.

(Waller, 2005)

In the past, a bank's investment customers relied on the bank to provide good returns and did not question the bank's lending policies. Increasingly today, investors are seeking socially responsible investments such as those offered by banks promoting themselves as 'ethical banks'. As Sparkes (2002) states, an 'ethical bank' refuses, for example, 'to lend or invest in companies that have poor environmental records... ' (p. 73) Investors in 'ethical, socially responsible and environmental funds include in their investment criteria judgments based on a moral assessment of what a business does ...' (Hancock, 2005, p. 41). However, as Hancock (op.cit.) also points out, 'It would not be socially responsible or, indeed, ethical to throw investors' money into businesses with little hope of success, however well meaning they may be.' (p. 45) There is a dilemma for the bank in balancing its customers' requests for socially responsible investments with its legitimate commercial needs.

Reference list

International Finance Corporation (n.d.). *Equator principles*. Retrieved July 7, 2007, from www.ifc.org/equatorprinciples

Langridge, K. (2006). 'Green' or ethical financial services set to become more mainstream. *Banking Business Review Online*. Retrieved September 20, 2007, from http://www.banking-business-review.com/article_feature.asp?guid=7D7281BF-3380-4192-BAA8-7CC878489B66

Sethi, S.P. (2005). Investing in socially responsible companies is a must for public pension funds - because there is no better alternative. *Journal of Business Ethics, 56*, 99–129.

Smith, R.C. and Walter, I. (2003). *Global banking*. (2nd Ed.). New York: Oxford University Press.

Vogel, D. (2006). *The market for virtue: the potential and limits of corporate social responsibility*. Washington D.C.: The Brookings Institution Press.

Case Studies in Sustainable Energy Projects

Brian Waller

Wentworth & Bourne

First published in 2005
by Wentworth & Bourne Ltd.
11 Vine Lane, London EC4P 5EI
© 2005 Brian Waller
Reprinted 2007

British Library Cataloguing-in-Publication Data
A catalogue record for this book is available from the British Library

Typeset by Glenda Graphics, Barnstaple, Devon, UK
Printed and bound by PW Enterprises, Bude, Cornwall, UK
ISBN 0-321-09487-3

Recognizing fixed phrases from banking (3)

Make sure you understand these key phrases from banking.

charity credit cards	lending criteria	operating costs	working capital
core business	lending practices	project finance	
Equator Principles	long-term	short-term	
financial instruments	medium-term	transaction fee	

Recognizing fixed phrases from academic English (3)

Make sure you understand these key phrases from general academic English.

One of the …   *In this sort of situation …*
In some circumstances, …   *It is obvious/clear that …*
Even so, …   *It appears to be the case that …*
… , as follows: …   *Research has shown …*
The writers conclude/assume/suggest that …   *The evidence does not support this idea.*

Recognizing levels of confidence in research or information

In an academic context, writers will usually indicate the level of confidence in information they are giving. When you read a 'fact' in a text, look for qualifying words before it, which show the level of confidence.

Examples:
Being tentative   *It appears to be the case that … / This suggests that …*
Being definite/confident   *The evidence shows that … / It is clear that …*

Recognizing 'marked' words

Many common words in English are 'neutral', i.e., they do not imply any view on the part of the writer or speaker. However, there are often apparent synonyms which are 'marked'. They show attitude, or stance.

Example:
*SRIs **rose** by 10% last year.*   *SRIs **soared** by 10% last year.*

Soared is marked because it implies that this is a particularly big or fast increase.

When you read a sentence, think: *Is this a neutral word, or is it a marked word? If it is marked, what does this tell me about the writer's attitude to the information?*

When you write a sentence, think: *Have I used neutral words or marked words? If I have used marked words, do they show my real attitude/the attitude of the original writer?*

Extend your vocabulary by learning marked words and their exact effect.

Neutral	Marked
go down, fall, decrease	slump, plummet
say, state	assert, maintain, claim, argue, allege
go up, rise, increase	soar, rocket
good	great, brilliant, tremendous

Identifying the parts of a long sentence

Long sentences often contain many separate parts. You must be able to recognize these parts to understand the sentence as a whole. Mark up a long sentence as follows:

- Locate the subjects, verbs and objects/complements and underline the relevant words.
- Put a dividing line:
  - at the end of a phrase which begins a sentence
  - before a phrase at the end of the sentence
  - between clauses.
- Put brackets round extra pieces of information.

Example:

In recent years many writers have claimed that high street banks are very positive in offering help to small entrepreneurs who request socially responsible investments.

In recent years | many <u>writers</u> have <u>claimed</u> | that high street <u>banks</u> are very <u>positive</u> in <u>offering</u> <u>help</u> to small <u>entrepreneurs</u> | (who request socially responsible investments).

Constructing a long sentence

Begin with a very simple SV(O)(C)(A) sentence and then add extra information.

Example:

	Banks		**offer**	**help.**		
Many writers have claimed that	*high street banks*	*are very positive*	*in offering*	*help*	*to small entrepreneurs*	*who request SRIs.*

Writing a bibliography/reference list

The APA (American Psychological Association) system is the most common in the social sciences. Information should be given as shown in the following source references for a book, an Internet article and a journal article. The final list should be in alphabetical order according to the family name of the writer. See the reference list on page 83 for a model.

Author	Date	Title of book	Place of publication	Publisher
Heffernan, S.	(2005).	*Modern banking.*	Chichester:	John Wiley & Sons

Writer or organization	Date (or 'n.d.')	Title of Internet article	Date of retrieval	Full URL
International Finance Corporation.	(n.d.)	*Equator Principles.*	Retrieved July 7, 2007 from	www.ifc.org/equatorprinciples business-review.com/

Author	Date	Title of article	Title of journal	Volume and page numbers
Robins, J.	(2006).	Social responsibility.	*Banker's Journal*	*18*, 74–98

More information on referencing (including other systems such as MLA) can be found on: http://owl.english.purdue.edu/owl/resource/560/10/ or www.westwords.com/guffey/apa.html

11.1 Vocabulary — linking ideas

A Look at the diagram on the opposite page.

  1 Name the factors.

  2 Discuss how the examples of each factor might influence banking.

  3 Give more examples of each factor.

B Study the linking words in box a.

  1 Put the linking words into two groups for:
    a discussing reasons and results
    b building an argument

  2 Is each linking word used to join ideas:
    a within a sentence
    b between sentences

  3 Can you think of similar linking words?

  4 Put the words in 1b in a suitable order to list points in support of an argument.

C Study the words in box b.

  1 Sort into three groups according to whether they are concerned with *people*, *money* or *change*.

  2 In pairs, explain your decisions.

  3 Are the words nouns, verbs or adjectives? What is their stress pattern?

  4 What other words or phrases have the same meaning?

D Read the text on the right.

  1 Complete each space with a word or phrase from box a or box b.

  2 Match the phrases below with a later phrase that refers back to them, as in the example:

    unexpectedly overdrawn

    banks cover the payment

    penalty rates

    Example:
    unexpectedly overdrawn – *insufficient funds*

  3 Can you think of other words with the same meaning as the blue words?

E Do the quiz on the opposite page.

---

a

Another point is …   As a result,   because
Finally,   Firstly,   For example,   In addition,
Moreover,   One result of this is …
Secondly,   since   So,

b

account holders   charges   consent   funds
insufficient   increasingly   keep track   manipulate
ombudsman   penalty rate   retain   rethink

In 2007, a large number of UK bank _____ complained to the financial _____ over penalty charges for going unexpectedly overdrawn. _____ , an inquiry was held by the Office of Fair Trading.

In the past, banks stopped payments from accounts with _____ funds, and charged the account owner a 'bounced-cheque' fee. However, payments today are _____ made as electronic transactions. _____ , instead of stopping payments from accounts with insufficient _____ , banks cover the payment. _____ that the customer is provided with an unauthorized overdraft. The bank _____ a fee on every subsequent transaction until the account is in funds.

The Consumer Federation of America (June 9, 2005) claims the _____ on overdrawn accounts are unfair, _____ they are extremely high. _____ , in the United States banks can legally _____ the order in which they pay debt transactions. _____ that the Federal Reserve does not consider overdraft fees as finance charges (which have to be disclosed). _____ , with an online account, the bank customer may see fees charged by the bank but no information on the basis for them.

Regardless of how a bank decides to post transactions, customers should _____ of their account balance, _____ going into overdraft is their responsibility. However, it could be argued that the banks need to _____ this policy if they want to _____ their customers. _____ , banks should obtain written _____ before providing an overdraft facility. _____ , a warning system could be installed so that customers know when there are insufficient funds for an ATM withdrawal. _____ , banks could allow time for cancelling the transaction.

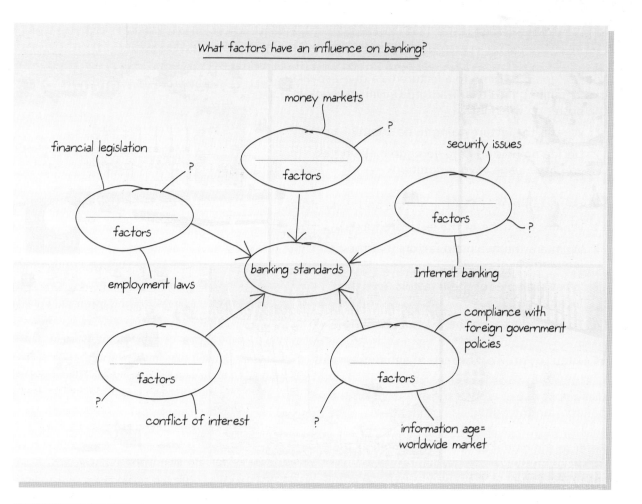

What factors have an influence on banking?

Banking quiz

What are the following and how do they relate to banking security?

1	ATM	8	pharming
2	biometrics	9	phishing
3	chip and PIN	10	proxy server
4	firewall	11	spyware
5	iris scan	12	Trojan horse
6	keylogger	13	two-factor ID
7	smart card	14	virus

A You are going to listen to a lecture by a guest speaker in the Banking faculty at Hadford University. Look at the poster on the right.

1 What is the lecture going to be about?

2 Decide on how you are going to make notes. Prepare a page in your notebook.

B 🎧 Now listen to Part 1 of the lecture and make notes.

1 What is the focus of the lecturer's talk?

2 What are the two main factors that the lecturer will discuss?

3 What examples of these factors does the lecturer give?

4 To which factor do the examples belong?

C 🎧 Listen to Part 2 of the lecture and make notes.

D Using your notes, answer the questions on the handout on the right.

E Refer to the model Cornell notes on page 105.

1 Check your answers with the model.

2 Complete the *Review* and *Summary* sections of the Cornell notes.

F The lecturer talks about security against ID theft.

1 Is biometric data recommended?

2 🎧 Listen again to part of the lecture. Which words tell us whether the information is fact or opinion?

G 🎧 Study the phrases below. Which type of information below follows each phrase in the blue box? Listen to some sentences from the lecture.

- restatement
- definite point
- reference to a source
- an example
- statement of a topic
- another point
- tentative point
- clarification
- purpose for speaking

H Write out one section of your notes in complete sentences.

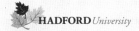

HADFORD *University*

Visiting Speaker: Dr John Hudson
15th February 5.00pm

'Maintaining banking standards in a global market: checks and balances'

Dr Hudson will explore key factors affecting banking standards in today's global environment.

---

1 What factor did the lecturer discuss first?

2 What examples of this factor did the lecturer mention?

3 What are two significant issues for banks?

4 How might banks deal with these issues?

5 What was the topic of the Unisys and Gartner Research surveys?

6 What are the solutions proposed for dealing with ID theft?

7 How have economic factors affected banking standards?

8 What affected global financial markets in 2007?

9 Who provided loans to banks with insufficient liquidity?

10 Name three important tools for banks in maintaining standards.

11 What type of behaviour does the code of conduct cover?

12 How does an ethics policy differ from a code of conduct?

---

1 that is to say

2 Don't misunderstand me.

3 It is fair to say that ...

4 not only that, but ...

5 in an attempt to ...

6 to the extent that ...

7 ... is a case in point

8 ... gives a good description

9 to some degree

10 There is no doubt that ...

11 Briefly the report explains how ...

12 with respect to ...

11.3 Extending skills
stresses in phrases • building an argument

A Study the phrases in box a.

1 Mark the stressed syllables in each phrase.

2 🎧 Listen and check your answers.

3 Check that you understand the meanings. Which phrases have adjective + noun? Which word has the stronger stress in these phrases?

B Look at the topics below.

inadequate regulation and supervision   fraud   security

1 What would you like to know about these topics?

2 Prepare a page in your notebook to make some notes.

3 🎧 Listen to Part 3 of the lecture and make notes. If there is information which you miss, leave a space.

4 Compare your notes with someone else. Fill in any blank spaces.

C Answer the questions on the Hadford University handout, using your notes.

D Study the stages of building an argument in box b.

1 Put the stages in an appropriate order.

2 Match each stage (a–e) with a phrase from box c.

E Look at box b and box c again.

1 🎧 Listen to some extracts from the lecture. Make notes of what the lecturer says for each stage of the argument (a–e).

2 Check your answers to exercises D and E1.

F Use your notes from this lesson to write 75–100 words about the main points in Part 3 of the lecture.

G In groups, discuss the research task set by the lecturer. Talk about these questions:

1 What are the three topics you need to consider?

2 Which one will you choose?

3 What ideas do you have about this topic already?

4 What kind of information will you need to find?

5 Where can you go to find more information?

Report back to the class on your discussion. In Lesson 4 you will take part in a seminar on this topic.

---

a
bank security
business opportunities
computer hacking
data protection
economic factors
ethics policy
globalization factors
unsolicited gifts

HADFORD *University*

1 What is the most serious economic issue, according to the lecturer?

2 What other factors affect this issue?

3 How does the lecturer define 'deregulation'?

4 What examples does the lecturer give of lenders making bad loan decisions?

5 What factors did *The Economist* describe as contributing to the 1997 Asian financial crisis?

6 Why do banks need robust financial controls?

7 How can banks remedy some of the problems discussed in the lecture?

8 What is your research task?

---

b
a giving a counter argument
b giving your opinion
c stating the issue
d supporting the reason with evidence
e rejecting a counter argument

---

c
It's quite clear that …
The question is …
I'm afraid … this just isn't true.
Some people claim …
The evidence lies in the fact that …

A Study the terms in box a.

  1 Explain the meaning of the terms.

  2 Mark the main stress in each term.

B Study the words in box b. Match the words to make phrases.

C Study web page **A** on the opposite page.

  1 Look at the section entitled 'Bank security products'. Describe each product.

  2 Look at the section entitled 'Customer security advice'. Which instruction is the most important? Why?

  3 Look at the section entitled 'Systems for secure transactions'. Describe each one.
Which of the systems should the bank use for networked PCs?

D Study the phrases in box c.

  1 What purpose would you use these phrases for in a seminar?

  2 Which phrases can you use for linking your new point to a contribution by another speaker?

E 🎧 Listen to some students taking part in a seminar. They have been asked to discuss initiatives for improving banking standards. While you listen, make a note of:

  1 the main topic of each extract

  2 the key details of each topic.

F Study web page **B** on the opposite page and discuss these questions:

  1 What is the main message on this page?

  2 Suggest two security measures.

  3 Why might banks be reluctant to implement these procedures?

G In groups, discuss your research findings on issues surrounding banking standards from Lesson 3. One person from the group should report the conclusions of the discussion to the class.

---

a

cheque account reconciliation
credit card transactions
due diligence processes
elder financial abuse
profit making objectives
transaction monitoring software

---

b

address	management
biometric	process
encryption	devices
laser	key
legitimate	profit
log	protection
notification	item
password	numbers
questionable	software
security	printer
serial	verification

---

c

I'd like to start by explaining …

To carry on from this first point, I want secondly to look at …

I don't think that is the main reason.

That seems like a very good point X is making.

I'm going to expand the topic by mentioning …

On the other hand, you might want to say that …

As well as this issue, we can also look at a very different issue.

So to sum up, we can say that …

Does anybody have any opinions or anything they would like to add?

I think we need a different viewpoint.

OK, to continue then …

Following on from what X has said …

(A)

BankSec.com the company that advises banks on Internet security issues

Look here for the latest regulations and information on:

Bank security products
- Chip and PIN cards
- Address verification system
- Smart cards
- Code checking
- Biometric devices
- Two-factor ID
- Security keys
- Encryption software

Systems for secure transactions
- Firewalls
- Anti-virus software
- Anti-spyware software
- Password protection
- Log management

Customer security advice
Educate your customers to:
- Keep their online password, user name and account security number safe, i.e., don't write them down!
- Report anything suspicious in their online account to the bank immediately.
- Use an effective anti-virus and appropriate malware detection software.
- Always log out by using the 'log out' button.
- Never leave their PC unattended when logged into their account.
- Never respond to e-mails requesting their security details.
- If they delete online financial information, make sure they purge the recycle bin by 'right-clicking' Empty Recycle Bin.
- When opening their online statement save it, or store it in a password-protected folder.

Staff training
Build good PC security habits:
- Run updated anti-virus programs frequently.
- Use anti-spyware and scan regularly, that is, at least monthly, and whenever something unusual is happening on your computer.

(B)

Online Bank Fraud

The advent of personal computers has increased Internet fraud, and laser printers have also substantially increased the incidents of cheque or desktop fraud. This is not only a threat to customer confidence but is also a significant cost to a banking business. By implementing procedures such as two-factor security, banks may reduce fraud significantly.

Banks need to look at how they can provide better security to reduce online bank fraud.
For advice on online bank security go to www.banksecurity.com.

Five types of bank fraud
1 elder financial abuse
2 cheque fraud
3 fraudulent loans
4 stolen credit cards
5 money laundering

Six types of online bank fraud
1 ID theft
2 phishing
3 Trojan horse
4 pharming
5 scamming
6 keylogging

Using words with similar meanings to refer back in a text

It is a good idea to learn several words with similar or related meanings. We often build cohesion in a text by using different words to refer back to something previously mentioned.

Examples:

First mention	Second mention	Third mention	Fourth mention
client	bank customer	account holder	saver/borrower
another jurisdiction	foreign country	another part of the world	another area
fewer	falling numbers of …	declining …	reduced …

Linking words

We use linking words to join ideas together in a sequence, to show how the ideas are related. Some linking words can be used to join independent and dependent clauses in a sentence.

Examples:

Information technology has revolutionized banking operations **because** it has increased efficiency.

OR

Because it has increased efficiency, information technology has revolutionized banking operations.

Other linking words join sentences in a text.

Example:

Many banks cover payments from accounts with insufficient funds. **As a result**, the customer is charged a penalty rate.

When building an argument, it is a good idea to use linking words to add points.

Firstly, …	Another point is …	In addition, …	… whereas …
For example, …	Secondly, …	Moreover, …	Finally, …

Recognizing fixed phrases from academic English (3)

In units 7 and 9, we learnt some key fixed phrases from general academic English. Here are some more to use when speaking.

Don't misunderstand me.	the history of …
I'm afraid that just isn't true.	the presence of …
in an attempt to …	there is a correlation between … and …
… is a case in point	to some degree …
not only that, but …	to the extent that …
Some people say …	What's more …
the effect of …	with respect to …

Writing out notes in full

When making notes we use as few words as possible. This means that when we come to write up the notes, we need to pay attention to:

- the use of symbols for words and ideas, e.g.,
  Notes: Gartner research → ID theft (2003-6) ↑ 50%
  Gartner research into ID theft showed a 50% increase between 2003 and 2006.

- making sure the grammatical words are put back in, e.g.,
  Notes: information technology → revolutionized banking operations
  Information technology has revolutionized banking operations.

- making the implied meanings clear, e.g.,
  Notes: biometrics - quality/ cost?
  There are quality and cost issues relating to the use of biometrics.

Building an argument

A common way to build an argument is:

1 First, state the issue.
  Can banks increase internal controls to reassure customers about security issues?

2 Next, give a counter argument.
  Robust internal controls would involve significant extra costs.

3 Then give your opinion.
  In fact, the benefits of increasing customer confidence would far outweigh the financial costs.

4 Then give evidence for your opinion.
  Studies have shown that customers will take their accounts to another bank if they are not satisfied with their current one.

Linking to a previous point

When you want to move the discussion in a new direction, introduce your comments with phrases such as:
Following on from what X said, I'd like to talk about …
I'm going to expand the topic by mentioning …
As well as X, we can also look at a very different sort of issue.

Summarizing a source

When we talk about the ideas of other people in a lecture or a seminar, we often give a summary of the source in a sentence or two.

Examples:
A book by (name of writer) *called* (name of book) *published in* (year) *gives an explanation of how …*
Briefly, (name of writer) *explains how …*
An introduction to (topic) *can be found in* (name of writer).

12 BANKING GOVERNANCE

12.1 Vocabulary

referring back • introducing quotations/paraphrases

A Study the words and phrases in box a.

  1 Check the meaning, stress and pronunciation.

  2 What part of speech is each word?

B Read text A on the opposite page.

  1 Replace the words and phrases in blue with a synonym from box b.

  2 Check the meaning, stress, pronunciation, and part of speech of the words in the text.

  3 Link each highlighted item to its noun.

  Example:

  they refers to previously mentioned noun (*banks*)

C Study the verbs in box c. They can be used to introduce quotations, paraphrases and summaries.

  1 Check the meanings of any words you don't know.

  2 Which verbs have similar meanings?

  3 Which verbs are not followed by *that*?

  4 When can you use each verb?

  Example:

  accept = agree but with some reluctance; the idea is often followed by *but*.

D Read text B on the opposite page. Look at the highlighted sentences.

  1 What is the purpose of each sentence?

  Example:

  Employees ... need to understand the specific provision of the law = opinion or recommendation.

  2 In an assignment, should you refer to the highlighted sentences by **quoting directly** or **paraphrasing**?

  3 Choose an appropriate introductory verb and write out each sentence as a direct quotation or a paraphrase. Add the source references.

E Look at the student notes on bank governance principles on the opposite page.

  1 Who should be responsible for creating a code of conduct?

  2 What does *best practice* mean?

  3 What does *arm's-length* mean?

  4 Who is responsible for defining risk areas?

---

a

accountability   compliance   corporate   explicit   fiduciary standards   implicit   integrity   observance   proactive   procedures   proliferation   provision

b

accepted practices   controlled by   dealt with   develop gradually   examination   guide   openness   problems   rules

c

accept   agree   argue   assert   cite   claim   concede   consider   contend   describe   disagree   dispute   emphasize   illustrate   indicate   insist   note   observe   point out   report   show   state   suggest

---

AZA Bank   internal memo

The recent audit has identified the following areas of internal control weaknesses:

1 Transactions with related parties (i.e., family members) which have been inappropriately authorized

2 Inadequate assessment of new financial products

3 Inadequate control over loan extensions

4

F Read the AZA Bank internal memo above. How should the bank respond to the governance issues identified in the audit?
For your answer, refer to the student notes in Exercise E.

A Bank governance

Because banks have the potential, if badly run, to create severe economic dysfunction, they are subject to strict regulations. The board of directors and senior management of the bank must ensure transparency and accountability govern their actions. They also have a responsibility to maintain high fiduciary standards, and consequently must implement strong governance procedures. Furthermore, these procedures need to be reviewed regularly, as banking standards and norms continue to evolve.

A significant part of governance is compliance. The main compliance risks should be identified and addressed annually by senior management. The bank can do this, by means of a regular review of its corporate governance practices and procedures. As part of this review, managers should carry out an 'internal audit' in which they examine their compliance with their risk management programs. As a result of such reviews, they should be able to identify the opportunities and threats to the bank.

From: James, D. (2007). *Analysing bank governance.* Hadford: Hadford University Press

B Managing compliance

Compliance has become a major responsibility for bank supervisors. Despite deregulation in the banking industry, there has been a proliferation of laws governing customer relationships. Compliance requires observance of those rules and regulations, both implicit and explicit, which govern bank procedures. As Robinson (2003) states, 'senior management are responsible for ensuring that … control processes are in place'.* All those involved in the day-to-day running of the bank, from the board members down, should be familiar with, and understand, the standards, rules and regulations that guide their work behaviour.

Employees throughout the bank need to understand the specific provision of the law as it applies to their own functions. In addition, they need to understand the intention of the law, so they can take a proactive approach to compliance in areas where no specific regulatory guidelines exist. This means anticipating the kinds of problems that, if not corrected, may lead to new compliance requirements.

*Robinson, D. (2003). FSA regulation of banking. Retrieved 30th Oct, 2006, from www.fsa.gov.uk/Pages/Library/Communication/Speeches/2003/sp138.shtml

From: Pickford, J. (2006). *Bank compliance issues.* Hadford: Hadford University Press.

Systems
- clearly defined responsibilities, decision-making authority, and accountability
- adequate checks and balances for approving and reviewing all transactions
- strong risk management functions and strong internal controls
- computer systems and procedures to safeguard security of information
- adequate customer documentation that meets public disclosure requirements

Customer relationships
- clear advice to customers on investment returns and risks
- compliance procedures to ensure that bank lending is on an arm's-length basis, and that credit extensions are effectively monitored
- limits set to restrict bank exposure to borrowers
- adequate policies and procedures to control international lending risks
- effective observance of 'know your customer' principles, and procedures to combat money-laundering activities

Internal responsibilities

Board of directors
- be people of integrity
- be accountable to shareholders
- set clear strategies to deal with significant risk
- define a code of conduct for all employees

Management
- promote a culture of trust, honesty and integrity within the organization
- define risk areas
- ensure the implementation of best practice in risk management

Staff
- possess skills and experience appropriate for their roles
- comply with bank's code of conduct
- exercise due diligence and integrity in performing their duties

A Discuss the following questions.

1 What risks do banks face when operating in other jurisdictions?

2 Who should take responsibility when problems occur?

B Read the title of the article on the opposite page. What will the text be about? Write three questions to which you would like answers.

C Read the text. Does it answer your questions?

D For each paragraph:

1 Identify the topic sentence.

2 Think of a suitable title.

E Look at the underlined words in the text. What do they refer back to?

F Study the highlighted words and phrases.

1 What do they have in common?

2 What linking words can you use to show:
- contrast?
- concession?
- result?
- reason?

3 Write the sentences with the highlighted items again, using other linkers with similar meanings.

G Read the sentences on the right. Number them 1–8 to show the order in which they happened.

H Read the text on the right. A student has written a summary of the first four paragraphs of the text about ABN AMRO but the quotations and paraphrases have not been correctly done. Can you spot the mistakes and correct them?

I Write a paragraph for a university lecturer, summarizing ABN AMRO's failure to comply with US banking regulations. Decide whether you should quote or paraphrase the material from the text.

	ABN AMRO bank voluntarily notified the US bank regulators, and De Nederlandesche Bank NV.
	On top of the financial penalties, ABN AMRO was required to implement additional compliance measures.
	ABN AMRO signed a 'written agreement' in July 2004 to improve its compliance procedures.
	ABN AMRO's auditors found non-compliance in its Dubai branch.
	ABN AMRO took action to improve controls based on the Basel principles.
	In 2005, the US regulators issued a cease-and-desist order, plus monetary penalties of US$75 million.
	Dubai branch employees modified payment instructions, allowing US dollar payments to be made to Iranians and Libyans.
1	US authorities identified non-compliance to some of their regulations by ABN AMRO bank.

As Robins (2005) explains that ABN AMRO's auditors identified violations of US regulations at its Dubai branch. It was not until after the bank signed a 'written agreement' with authorities in the US that the Dubai problems were found. According to Robins, she says that ABN AMRO <u>voluntarily</u> notified US banking authorities then fining the Dutch bank US$75 million.

The Bankers' Journal

ABN AMRO Bank
– A case study in failure to take account of compliance issues
By Jane Robins

In July 2004, ABN AMRO, the large international bank, signed a so-called 'written agreement' with US regulatory authorities concerning ABN AMRO's dollar clearing activities in its New York branch. The written agreement related to non-compliance with the US Bank Secrecy Act and the US Treasury Department's Office of Foreign Assets Control (OFAC) regulations, and identified deficiencies in ABN AMRO's anti-money laundering policies, procedures and practices. In response to the written agreement, ABN AMRO improved its compliance function and anti-money laundering program in New York.

ABN AMRO headquarters in the Netherlands

However, ABN AMRO's auditors identified violations of US regulations coming from its Dubai branch. It was discovered that certain employees of the Dubai branch, without the knowledge of anyone outside the branch, had not been observing the bank's policies and standards relating to US dollar payment instructions. Between 1997 and 2004, Dubai branch employees had modified payment instructions which had been sent to ABN AMRO's US dollar clearing house in New York, on behalf of Libyan and Iranian clients. Although ABN AMRO bank, under European Union legislation, was allowed to deal with Libya and Iran, in the US these countries were on the list of the OFAC's sanctioned countries. Consequently, payments involving nationals of these countries had to meet specific OFAC requirements before they could be cleared in the US. However, employees at ABN AMRO's Dubai branch had excluded or modified the client-specific information from the relevant payment instructions to the New York clearing centre. This meant they would not be detected and blocked as they passed through the OFAC's filter.

ABN AMRO stopped these procedures once they were detected. In addition, it took disciplinary measures, including terminations, against the employees involved. The bank also confirmed that there was no evidence of terrorist connections with the transactions. Despite the fact that ABN AMRO bank had voluntarily notified the US banking authorities and De Nederlandesche Bank NV (the regulator of Dutch banks), the authorities decided that further enforcement action was required. Therefore, on December 19, 2005, the regulators issued a cease-and-desist order against ABN AMRO and its branches in New York and Chicago. They also assessed civil monetary penalties against ABN AMRO totalling US$75 million, plus an additional US$5 million voluntary payment to the Illinois Bank Examiners' Education Foundation.

On top of the financial penalties, ABN AMRO was required to implement additional compliance measures. In a press release (dated December 19, 2005) the chairman of ABN AMRO's managing board asserted that he was committed to ensuring that its implementation of a compliance function within the bank

'would achieve the highest standards in this area and serve as a benchmark for the entire financial industry.' The bank also stated that it had implemented a large number of measures in the area of worldwide compliance, based on the Basel principles. These principles set out broad supervisory standards and guidelines, and provide recommendations of best practice in banking supervision. The most recent guidelines, contained in the Basel Capital Accord (Basel II), are designed to promote greater consistency in the way banks and banking regulators approach risk management across national borders. While implementation is voluntary, all the 13 member countries of the Basel Committee on Banking Supervision, together with 82 of 98 non-member countries surveyed in 2006, plan to implement Basel II.

The ABN AMRO case has demonstrated that central banks and regulating agencies consider inadequate controls and serious non-compliance issues to be totally unacceptable. Non-complying institutions risk not only heavy penalties, but serious damage to their reputations. ∎

A Study the words in box a.

1 Check the pronunciation and grammar.

2 What are their meanings in a research report?

B Read the introduction to Report A and the conclusion to Report B, on the opposite page.

1 What methods were used in each piece of research?

2 What are the elements of a good introduction and conclusion?

C Read the two *method* paragraphs on the right.

1 Copy them into your notebooks. Put the verbs in brackets in the correct form.

2 Identify the original research questions, the research methods and other important information.

D What are the sections of a research report? What order should they go in?

Report A: Method

A written questionnaire (*design*) to find out the likely cost of implementing Basel II and the year institutions expected to be fully compliant. An online survey (*carry out*) of 102 senior executives in mid-tier banks. In addition, senior executives (*interview*) at a number of banks.

Report B: Method

In order to find out how many countries intended to implement Basel II, a questionnaire (*send out*) during 2006. The 13 member countries of the Basel Committee on Banking Supervision (*question*). In addition, 115 non-member countries (*include*).

A Describe the data in Figures 1 and 2 on the opposite page.

B Look at the *findings* section of Report A on the right.

1 Complete the spaces with quantity phrases. Put the verbs in the correct tense.

2 Write another paragraph, using Figure 2.

C Write a discussion paragraph for report B using the ideas from the research notes on the opposite page.

Report A: Findings

Firstly, on the negative side, _____ (79%) of respondents (*say*) that they were not sure when they would be fully compliant. Only _____ (1.1%) (*state*) that they did not expect to be fully compliant until 2011 or later. Although 7% _____ the respondents (*think*) that they would be fully compliant by 2009 and 2010, over 17% (*state*) they would be fully compliant in 2007.

Report A Introduction

The Basel II Capital Accord is a comprehensive framework for determining regulatory capital requirements and measuring risk. It aims to help banks and financial systems become more resilient to a rapidly changing world financial environment. However, a criticism of the accord has been the cost of implementation, so it is important to find out whether this will lead to delays in its introduction, particularly among mid-tier banks. This report will describe a survey of mid-tier banks undertaken in 2004, to find out when they expect to be fully compliant with the Basel II accord. The research also aims to identify whether implementation costs will impact compliance.

Report B Conclusion

To conclude, 82 of the total number of 98 respondents state that they intend to adopt the Basel II accord. The other 16 respondents do not indicate why they are not adopting the accord. However, the cost of implementation is likely to be a factor for less wealthy economies.

It is clear that *all* countries should be encouraged to adopt the accord. Unless there is universal adoption of the recommendations, there is the risk that smaller banks, and those in less developed regions, will be unable to participate in a global banking economy. However, if the problems facing less wealthy economies can be accommodated, then the implementation of Basel II will ensure greater consistency and soundness in banking and financial standards globally.

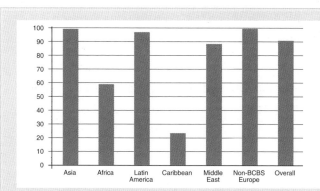

Figure 1: *Percentage of non-member countries planning to adopt Basel II, shown by region*
Source: Basel Committee on Banking Supervision

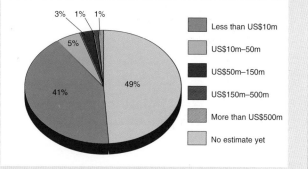

Figure 2: *Estimated cost of implementation of Basel II by percentage of respondents*
Source: http://www.oracle.com/industries/campaigns/finsrv/oracle_eiu_baselii.pdf

Report B
Research notes on compliance to Basel II
1. Member countries

Country	Compliance expected	Comments
USA	2009	only top 10-20 banks
		mid-tier and other banks apply Basel I
EU	2007-2008	some banks on Basel I until 2008
Japan	2008	

2. Non-member countries (>100 expected by 2010)
Asia Pacific

Country	Compliance expected	Comments
Australia	2008	sophisticated banks
China	no timetable	intention = adopt in principle
India	to be announced	intention = adopt in principle
Indonesia	2011	

Introductory verbs

Choosing the right introductory verb is important. Your choice of introductory verb shows what kind of statement the writer is making.

Example:
Pickford (2006) suggests that employees should understand how the law 'applies to their own functions'.

Your choice of introductory verb also shows what you think of another writer's ideas. This is an important part of academic work.

Example:
Pickford (2006) claims that, in banking compliance, implicit and explicit rules must be followed.

Verb	The writer …
agree	thinks this idea from someone else is true
accept, concede	reluctantly thinks this idea from someone else is true
consider, emphasize, note, observe, point out, state, suggest*	is giving his/her opinion
argue, assert, claim, contend, insist	is giving an opinion that others may not agree with
cite	is referring to someone else's ideas
disagree, dispute	thinks an idea is wrong
suggest*	is giving his/her recommendation
describe	is giving a definition/description
illustrate, indicate, show	is explaining, possibly with an example
report	is giving research findings

*suggest can have two meanings

Linking ideas in a text

Linking words, which join ideas within a sentence or between sentences, convey different meanings.

	Within sentences	Between sentences
Contrast	*but, whereas, while*	*However, In/By contrast, On the other hand*
Concession	*although, despite/ in spite of the fact that*	*However, At the same time, Nevertheless, Despite/In spite of + noun, Yet*
Result	*so, so that*	*So, As a result, Consequently, Therefore*
Reason	*because, since, as*	*Because of + noun, Owing to + noun, Due to + noun*

Referring to quantities and group sizes in a report

A/An	*overwhelming/large/significant slight/small/insignificant/tiny*	*majority*	
		minority	
		number	*(of + noun)*
Over		*half*	
More	*than*	*a quarter*	
		a third	
Less		*x %*	

Structuring a research report

A research report is an account of some research which has been undertaken to find out about a situation or a phenomenon, e.g., *When does your institution expect to be fully compliant with Basel II?*

- Introduction   introduce topic; background information; reasons for research
- Methods   research questions; how research was carried out
- Findings/results   answers to research questions
- Discussion   issues arising from findings; limitations of research
- Conclusion   summary of main findings; implications; recommendations; possibilities for further research

Writing introductions and conclusions

Introduction

- Introduce the topic of the report.
- Say why the topic is important.
- Give background information.
- Give an outline of the report plan.

Note: No substantial information; this belongs in the body of the report.

Conclusion

- Summarize the main points in the report without repeating unnecessarily.
- Make some concluding comments such as likely implications or recommendations.

Note: No new information; all the main points should be in the body of the report.

Deciding when to quote and when to paraphrase

When referring to sources, you will need to decide whether to quote directly or to paraphrase/summarize.

- **Quote** when the writer's words are special or show a particularly clever use of language. This is often the case with strongly stated *definitions* or *opinions*.
- **Paraphrase**/summarize descriptions and factual information.

Incorporating quotations

- Use an introducing verb.
- Don't forget the quotation marks.
- Make the quote fit the grammar of the sentence.
- Show any missing words with '…'.
- Copy the original words exactly.
- Add emphasis with italics and write [italics added].

Additional material
5.3 Symbols and abbreviations for notes

Symbols

&, +	and, plus
−	less, minus
±	plus or minus
=	is, equals, is the same as
≈	is approximately equivalent to
≠	is not, is not the same as, doesn't mean, does not equal, is different from
>	is greater than, is more than, is over
<	is less than
→	gives, produces, leads to, results in
←	is given by, is produced by, results from, comes from
↑	rises, increases, grows
↓	falls, decreases, declines
"	ditto (repeats text immediately above)
∴	therefore, so
∵	because, as, since
≅	at
C	century, as in 20th C
§	paragraph
#	number, as in #1
?	this is doubtful

Abbreviations

e.g.	for example
c.	approximately, as in c.1900
cf.	compare
Ch.	chapter
ed./eds	editor(s)
et al.	and the other people (used when referring to a book with more than one author)
etc.	and all the rest
ff.	and the following as in p.10ff.
fig.	figure (used when giving a title to a drawing or table)
i.e.	that is, that means, in other words
ibid.	in the same place in the source already mentioned
NB	important
No., no.	number
op.cit.	in the source already mentioned
p.	page
pp.	pages, as in pp.1–10
re.	concerning
ref.	with reference to
viz.	namely
vol.	volume

5.4 Group B

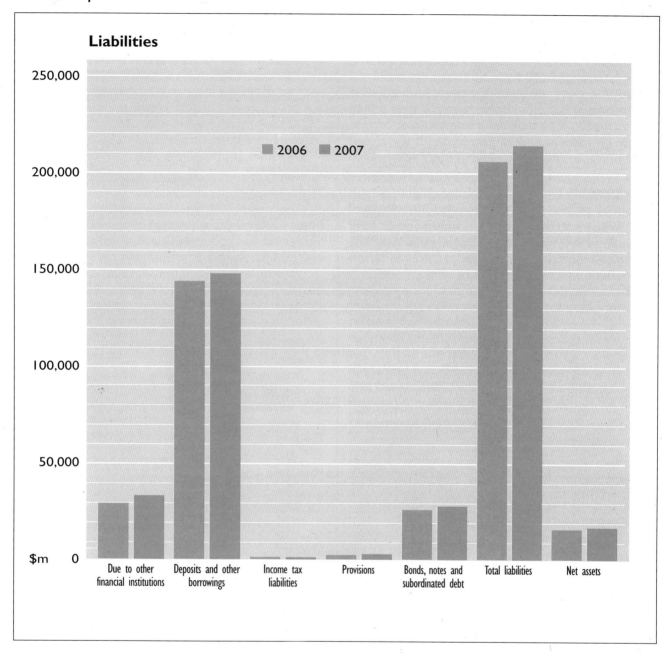

Liabilities

| | 2006 | 2007 |

(bar chart showing liabilities in $m, y-axis from 0 to 250,000)

Categories: Due to other financial institutions, Deposits and other borrowings, Income tax liabilities, Provisions, Bonds, notes and subordinated debt, Total liabilities, Net assets

7.4 Student A

Payment method	cash with order (CWO)
Payment to exporter	when order is placed, prior to shipment
Title/goods available to importer	depends on contract specification, e.g., ex factory, FOB (free on board), on delivery, or on acceptance after arrival
Bank involvement	importer may require finance
Risk to importer	if exporter doesn't adhere to contract terms
Risk to exporter	very little
Not advised if/when	trading partner is a government or an established trading partner – implies lack of trust

5.4 Group C

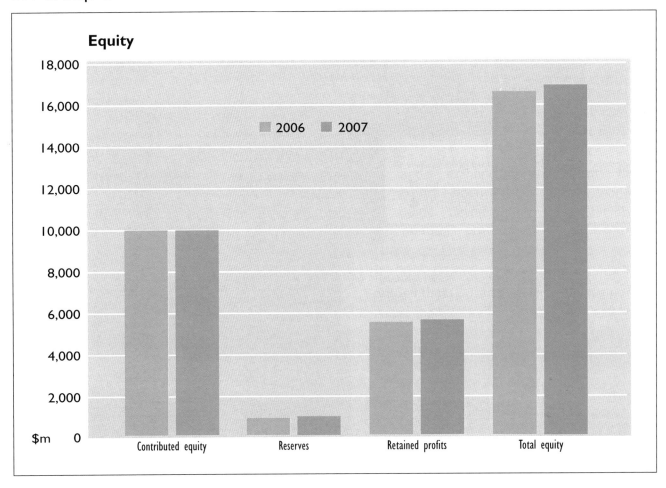

7.4 Student B

Payment method	**letter of credit (L/C)** • used for business transactions in which the payment of the invoice needs to be guaranteed by a third party (usually a bank), e.g., if buyer's country is economically/politically unstable • can be denominated in a stable currency, e.g., USD, euro
Payment to exporter	on submission of documents under L/C after goods arrive safely
Title/goods available to importer	when letter of credit is settled
Bank involvement	L/C is drawn by the exporter's bank on the importer's bank which promises to honour it (by confirming it) if the exporter meets the terms in it
Risk to importer	• if exporter doesn't adhere to the contract terms • possibility of fraud
Risk to exporter	• very little for a confirmed irrevocable L/C if documents comply • exporter may require FX (foreign exchange) contract to guarantee price received for the goods (if there is the potential for currency fluctuations)
Not advised if/when	• importing country is politically unstable, i.e., risk that movement of funds out will be stopped (in event of war, etc.) • profit margin is low as L/C involves added costs • goods are perishable as L/C is time-consuming

11.2 Model Cornell notes

Review	Notes
	1 <u>Technological factors:</u>
	a) information technology
	$\longrightarrow$ revolutionized banking operations:
	• efficiency
	• new services, e.g., Internet banking
	$\longrightarrow$ compromised bank security:
	• Internet fraud (phishing, pharming, spyware)
	b) key issues: data protection and privacy
	$\longrightarrow$ client education
	$\longrightarrow$ staff with technical expertise
	c) ID theft
	• Unisys research $\longrightarrow$ (2005) 17% US, 11% UK consumers = victims
	• Gartner research $\longrightarrow$ ID theft (2003-6) $\uparrow$ 50%
	Proposed solutions:
	• biometrics - quality/ cost?
	• 2-factor ID, i.e., password + mobile phone confirmation
	• US Dept. Justice $\longrightarrow$ appropriate penalties; computer fraud illegal
	2 <u>Other factors</u>
	• economic $\longrightarrow$ conflicts of interest
	• globalization: events in one country influence world markets, e.g., 2007 US sub-prime mortgage defaults $\longrightarrow$ central banks (US, Europe, Japan, England) = lenders of last resort to banks with insufficient liquidity
	• bad practice: BNZ (2006) $\longrightarrow$ unrealistic sales targets $\longrightarrow$ employee stress $\longrightarrow$?non-compliance with banking standards
	<u>How to maintain banking standards?</u>
	• code of conduct $\longrightarrow$ specific info on acceptable business behaviour
	• departmental procedures $\longrightarrow$ specific step-by-step instructions
	• ethics policy $\longrightarrow$ expresses bank's underlying values See World Bank Code of Ethics
	○ unpredictable situations in day-to-day operations
	○ relationships $\longrightarrow$ person to person, workplace, bank's relationship with outside community

Summary:

7.4 Student C

Payment method	**documentary collection** equal risk/benefit to both parties; used when parties have an established relationship and know each other well
Payment to exporter	on acceptance of bill of exchange
Title/goods available to importer	on payment or acceptance of bill of exchange by importer's bank (on behalf of the importer)
Bank involvement	exporter sends title documents (bill of exchange, bill of lading, etc.) through own bank to importer with instruction to release them to importer on acceptance/payment of bill of exchange
Risk to importer	• fraud or misunderstanding regarding goods • loss of goods
Risk to exporter	possibility of importer not accepting the bill of exchange
Not advised if/when	• importing country has weak economy or if unstable politically, e.g., it may place restrictions on foreign currency payments • it is a government order, as payment is not released until goods are certified by government agency, i.e., goods handed over (for certification) before payment

7.4 Student D

Payment method	**cash on delivery (COD)** exporter ships goods and sends commercial documents to buyer directly
Payment to exporter	after delivery of the goods, if importer satisfied with conditions of the delivery, and quantity and quality of the goods
Title/goods available to importer	on delivery
Bank involvement	• exporter may require normal working capital finance, particularly if the order is a large one • both importer and exporter may wish to take out a FX contract
Risk to importer	fraud or misunderstanding regarding goods
Risk to exporter	exporter loses all control over goods and depends on the buyer to make payment as per contract
Not advised if/when	importer and exporter are not well known to each other and don't have an established trading relationship

Wordlist

Note: Where a word has more than one part of speech, this is indicated in brackets. The part of speech given is that of the word as it is used in the unit. So, for example, *bond* is listed as *bond (n)*, although it can also be a verb.

A	Unit
access (n and v)	4, 8
account (n)	1, 5
account holders	11
accountability	12
accumulated	5
acquisition	9
advance (n and v)	2
analysis	5
anonymity	8
appreciate	6
appreciation	6
asset	2, 5, 8
ATM	1
authorities (pl n)	8
authorize	7

B	Unit
balance (n)	2
(bank)note	2
bankrupt (adj and n)	1, 2
bankruptcy	2
basket	6
bearer	2
bill of exchange	2, 7
biometric	11
bond (n)	2
borrower	2
bounced cheque	11
branch	1
browse	4
building society	3
buyer	7

C	Unit
capital	6, 10
cash on delivery	7
cash with order	7

	Unit
central bank	1, 3
charity credit cards	10
charter (n and v)	2
check (AmE)	1
cheque (BrE)	1
circulation	1, 2
client	1
code of conduct	11
commercial bank	1
compatible	4
compliance	11, 12
computer hacking	11
computerize	4
conflict of interest	11
conglomerate	3
consolidation	9
control (n)	8, 12
convertible	1
core business	10
correlate	6
counterfeit	2
credit (n and v)	1, 2, 7
credit (n)	1
credit rating	7
creditor	1
creditworthy	7
currency	1, 2
currency fluctuations	7

D	Unit
data	4
database	4
data protection	11
debt	5
debtor	1
declaration	8
declare	8
default (n and v)	7, 11

	Unit
deficit	5
deflation	6
delivery	7
deposit (n and v)	1, 2
depreciation	1
deregulation	11
disclosure	8
distributed	5
diversification	9, 11
dividend	3
document (n)	4, 7
documentary collection	7
due diligence	11
dysfunction	12

E	Unit
e-banking	4
economic indicator	9
electronic media	4
emerging market	9
encryption software	11
Equator Principles	10
equity	3, 5
ethics	10
ethics policy	11
expenses	5
explicit	12
export (n and v)	7
exporter	7

F	Unit
fiduciary	12
finance (n and v)	2, 10
financial	1, 2
financial instruments	10
financial liberalization	9
fix (v)	1
fixed	1

	Unit		Unit		Unit
online banking	3	registration	8	sub-prime mortgage	11
onshore	8	regulate	1, 2, 6	sub-regional	9
open account terms	7	regulation	1, 2, 6, 7, 8, 11	supervisory	12
operating	5	regulatory	1, 10, 12	surplus (n and adj)	5
operating costs	10	reserve (n and v)	2, 6		
order (n and v)	7	residence	8	**T**	
output (n and v)	4	resident	8	tangible	5
overdrawn	11	restriction	8	target (n and v)	6
over-the-counter	8	restructuring	9	tax evasion	8
ownership	6	retail bank	1	tax haven	8
		retain	8	taxation	8
P		retained	5	technology	11
password	4, 11	return (n)	1, 8	telephone banking	3
payable	1	revenue	5	term	1, 7
payment terms	7	risk (n and v)	7	text message banking	3
penalty rate	11			touch-screen share dealing	3
per capita income	9	**S**		trade services	3
performance	5	savings	1	transaction fee	10
personal loan	3	scamming	11	transaction	1, 2, 4
pharming	11	screening	8	transfer (n and v)	1, 4
phishing	11	search (n and v)	4	transparency	10, 12
policy	6	search engine	4	Trojan horse	11
pre-shipment	7	search results	4	two-factor ID	11
privacy	8	securities	3		
privatization	9	security	1, 7, 11	**U**	
privatize	9	serial numbers	11	username/ID	4
proactive	12	share capital	3		
procedure	12	shipment	7	**V**	
profit margin	7	short-term	10	variable	1
project finance	10	slump (n and v)	10	vault (n)	2
proliferation	12	smart card	11	verification	11
promissory note	2	socially responsible			
protection	11	investment (SRI)	10	**W**	
provision	5, 12	software	4	wholesale bank	1
proxy server	11	source country	9	withdraw	2
		specification	4	withdrawal	2
R		spyware	11	working capital	10
rate (n)	1	stability	6		
recall (v)	1	stable (adj)	6		
receipt	2, 7	statement	5		
reconciliation	11	stock (n)	6		

Transcripts

Unit 1, Lesson 2, Exercise B 🎧 1.1

Part 1

Welcome to 'An introduction to banking'. What do we mean by the term banking? We all associate banking with banks, of course, so let's start there. The English word bank has 13th-century origins in both German and Italian. When you hear the word bank you generally think of money … right? But actually, the word bank is derived from the Italian word *banca*, which evolved from a German word meaning bench. What has banking got to do with benches? Well, in the past, Italian moneylenders used a bench or table in a large open area to conduct their business. So the word originally referred to the place where money-lending transactions occurred.

Today the word bank refers to the institution which carries out banking services. It also refers to a building where banking services are provided. That is, the offices or buildings in which a bank is located. It can also be a verb: we can say 'Who do you bank with?'

Incidentally, the English term bankrupt is used to describe a person who has gone out of business because they could not meet all their liabilities. This term comes from the expression *banca rotta*, meaning a physically broken bench.

The English words cash, debtor, creditor, ledger, and the symbols for English currency, pounds and pence, all originate from the 13th century, too.

Unit 1, Lesson 2, Exercise C 🎧 1.2

Part 2

So, we agree that banking is about money. But finance is also about money. Does this mean that banking and finance are the same? Not really. Banks are financial institutions, but so are insurance companies and investment companies. Some financial institutions provide banking services, but they cannot be defined as a bank. Why not? Because they do not fulfil the legal definition of a bank. In Britain, all financial institutions are controlled by the Financial Services Authority, or FSA. There is legislation covering the services provided by each institution. A bank is a government-licensed institution. It is established under a government charter. A banking license gives the right to conduct banking services, particularly services related to the storing, or keeping, of deposits, and the extending, or offering, of credit.

Unit 1, Lesson 2, Exercise D 🎧 1.3

Part 3

Banks can be categorized into wholesale banks, retail banks, and central banks. It's a bit more complicated than that in reality, but those are the main categories. Both wholesale and retail banks provide the three essential functions of deposits, payments and credits, which are the basis of their services. Wholesale banks, which include merchant banks, provide large-scale services to companies, government agencies and other banks. Retail banks, on the other hand, mainly provide smaller-scale services to the general public. These banks include the trading or commercial banks, and savings banks.

The main government-controlled bank in a country, the central bank, fixes the main interest rates, issues currency, supervises commercial banks and tries to control foreign exchange.

As I mentioned earlier, the term bank is generally understood as an institution that holds a banking license. Banking licenses are granted by bank regulatory authorities and provide rights to conduct the most fundamental banking services such as accepting deposits and making loans. Banks generate income through charging interest on loans and charging transaction fees on their financial services.

In the US, banks are under the jurisdiction of the central bank of the United States – the Federal Reserve Bank. In the United Kingdom the central bank is the Bank of England.

Unit 1, Lesson 2, Exercise E 🎧 1.4

Part 4

The roles and functions of banks have evolved and changed over the years. Today, the variety of services that a bank offers depends on the type of bank, and the country. Many of the larger banks offer services outside those traditionally associated with banking. They may deal in financial instruments such as share certificates, certificates of deposit, and bills of exchange. A financial instrument is a legal document. It shows that money has been lent or borrowed, invested or passed from one account to another.

Some banks also offer banking and insurance to their customers, hence the term bancassurer. Notice the spelling, with a *c* not a *k*. However, the essential function of a bank is to provide services relating to the storing and management of money for its customers. These services include most or all of the following: accepting demand and time deposits and paying interest on them, making loans and charging interest on them, investing in securities, issuing bank drafts and cheques, accepting cheques, drafts and notes.

Banks also provide other banking services including deposit facilities, leases, mortgages, credit cards, ATM networks, securities brokerage, investment banking, mutual and pension funds, and so on.

Banking can be defined, therefore, as the management of financial instruments and money, in the form of time deposits, securities, bank drafts, cheques, etc., within the context of specific national legislation.

Unit 1, Lesson 3, Exercise E 🎧 1.5

Introduction 1

Today we'll look at the globalization of private banking. In particular, we'll look at the advantages and disadvantages of foreign banks coming into a country. In recent years, we have seen a worldwide expansion of MNBs, or multinational banks. In many of the less developed nations, branches or subsidiaries of foreign commercial banks dominate the banking system. Incidentally, you may like to note that a subsidiary is independent of the parent bank, whereas a branch is not.

Introduction 2

My topic today is the organizational structure of banks. This is important, because it affects the way a bank operates. I am going to consider the effects of centralization on various aspects of bank management, including authority, accountability, decision-making and leadership. For each element, I'm going to compare the two approaches – centralized or decentralized.

Introduction 3

Today I want to consider the question 'Why are banks regulated?' There are a number of reasons for this. I am going to look at five of these. Firstly, there is the economic role of banks; secondly, the need to protect customers; thirdly, the prevention of a banking collapse, and the central bank's role in this; and fourthly, the competition issue. Finally, there is the issue of the scope of banking activities. What can banks actually do? Let's consider each point in turn.

Introduction 4

OK. Are we all ready? Is everyone here? We seem to have a small class today, so feel free to interrupt me if you have any questions. Right, I'll begin. For centuries, bankers have attempted to establish a global monetary regime or monetary standard. By this I mean the establishing of a fixed exchange rate for a currency. Today we're going to look at key developments in establishing a global monetary standard over the last 200 years or so.

Introduction 5

In this week's lecture, I'm going to discuss some aspects of modern technology and banking. Computers and other electronic machines are widely used in retail banking – for example, in the processing of cheques. A cheque is presented at a bank and an electronic procedure begins. The bank teller enters the details of the cheque onto the system. The computer reads the magnetic code. Money is debited from the payer's account electronically. The cheque is then sent to the clearing house and money is then credited to the payee's account.

Let's look at some more electronic procedures.

Unit 1, Lesson 4, Exercise D 🎧 1.6

Lecture 1

There are advantages and disadvantages of foreign bank participation in a national banking market. Of course, one advantage for MNBs is cost: operating costs are often lower in the other country. But there can be advantages for the country in which they are operating, too. One advantage of foreign participation is that it often increases the efficiency of the domestic banks. How can this happen? Well, businesses are often inefficient in a market with little or no competition. When an MNB comes into this kind of market, competition increases and, sometimes, the efficiency of domestic banks increases as a result. However, on the other hand, the arrival of an MNB may be unwelcome competition for other domestic banks. The profitability of domestic banks may go down.

Another problem posed by cross-border banks is that of financial guarantees from the parent bank in the event of a failure in the local branch or subsidiary. The issues that need to be resolved in the event of a crisis in a subsidiary bank include: whose responsibility is it to handle such a crisis? What role should the host nation authorities play? And finally, given that the host nations are often the smaller nations, are they able to handle a crisis of a large cross-border bank?

Unit 1, Lesson 4, Exercise D 🎧 1.7

Lecture 2

Let's start with authority. A centralized bank keeps its authority at the top level, whereas a decentralized bank delegates some authority to lower levels. As a result, accountability in a centralized bank should stay at the top level, whereas some accountability may be delegated in a decentralized bank. Of course, ultimately accountability will lie with the highest level of management in either situation.

The decision to be centralized or not can have a significant effect on growth. A small organization can work effectively in a centralized mode, but, as a bank grows, a decentralized organization may be more effective. The main reason for this is that if decisions don't have to go through a long chain of command, decision-making can be quicker. In a rapidly changing or uncertain environment, a decentralized organization is often more effective.

It allows the bank to react quickly to changing circumstances. It can also be more flexible.

Centralized decision-making, on the other hand, is more effective in a stable environment. It allows more co-ordination in the organization. It also allows greater influence of leadership from the top.

Unit 1, Lesson 4, Exercise D 🎧 1.8

Lecture 3

So, firstly, banks have an important role in the economy of a country. No government can afford to allow the banking system to fail. Therefore, governments maintain regulatory controls over bank operations. For example, they implement exchange controls. These restrict the amount of local currency that can be changed into foreign currencies.

Secondly, the regulations are there to protect the bank's customers. In the event of a bank failure it's important to make sure that small depositors don't lose their savings.

The third point relates to the need to prevent banking collapse. An important objective of bank regulation has been the prevention of a recession, or serious decline in the country's economy. This can occur when thousands of people have become bankrupt or unemployed. A bankrupt is a person whose affairs have been put into receivership, because they have been legally declared incapable of paying their debts.

In the 1930s, a 'bank run' occurred in the United States. Customers rushed to withdraw their deposits from banks which they thought were closing down. A consequence of bank runs is that they can spread to financially healthy banks, and this can have a serious impact on a country's economy.

The banking regulation set up to prevent such an occurrence is the 'lender of last resort' function. This is the ultimate source of credit to which banks can turn. In the United States, the Federal Reserve was created to serve as the 'lender of last resort'. However, it failed in that role during the Great Depression. Generally, the role of 'lender of last resort' falls to the central bank of a country. For example, in the UK it is the Bank of England, which lends money to commercial banks. And in fact, in 2007, the Bank of England did step in to lend money to Northern Rock during the so-called 'credit crunch'.

Because of the failure of the Federal Reserve Bank in its 'lender of last resort' function in the 1930s, the United States set up the Federal Deposit Insurance Corporation. By charging banks a standard premium on their deposits, the FDIC insures deposits in commercial banks and in savings and loan associations.

What's the fourth point? Oh, yes, competition. Legislative restrictions have also been placed on banking industry competition. In the United States until recently, there were 'branching restrictions'. These limited the ability of banks to expand outside their regions or states. However, the branching restrictions didn't apply to bank holding companies. These are firms that own many different banks as subsidiaries.

Finally, many countries place restrictions on the scope of bank activities. For example, banks are not allowed to engage in non-financial activities. Also, different types of banks may be restricted in the type of services they can provide. The purpose of bank regulations is to provide stability in the banking system.

Unit 1, Lesson 4, Exercise D 🎧 1.9

Lecture 4

LECTURER: Early in the 19th century, Britain wanted to standardize the value of its currency, so the country adopted the gold standard for the British pound. Until that time, the value of the pound (or pound sterling) was based on an amount of silver in that weight. However, after the gold standard was adopted, the mint produced gold, instead of silver, coins. The mint, of course, is the factory where the government makes money. Almost half a century later, when the German states merged into one country, they also adopted the gold standard. They were followed by the Scandinavian countries, then France and Japan. Although there was an enormous increase in gold supplies, with new discoveries in Alaska, Africa and Australia, the United States didn't officially adopt the gold standard until 1900.

Between 1880 and 1930, the gold standard, which defined a national currency in terms of a fixed weight of gold, became the most common monetary arrangement, allowing a global fixed exchange rate system. Some people believe it contributed to a period of globalization and economic modernization. However, at the start of the First World War, Britain withdrew gold from internal circulation, and after the depression of the 1930s, the gold standard was abandoned by most countries as a monetary policy.

STUDENT: Excuse me, but wasn't there a recent attempt to back currency with gold, in one of the Asian countries? Why wasn't it successful?

LECTURER: Yes, there was an attempt to produce a gold currency, in 2001. Prime Minister Mahathir of Malaysia proposed a new currency of 425 grams of gold, to be called the gold dinar. Prime Minister Mahathir thought there were good economic reasons for having a gold currency, and he also believed it would be a unifying symbol for Islamic nations, who would use it for their trade. But then Mahathir resigned as prime minister, and his proposal wasn't taken any further.

So, where was I? Oh, yes, for a period of time, between the wars, the pound sterling became the key global currency. Then, following the Second World War, it was replaced by the United States dollar.

STUDENT: Can I ask what has replaced the gold standard? I mean, how are currencies valued today?

LECTURER: Most governments manage money by regulating their economy or the money supply.

They also peg their currencies to a currency board. By currency board, I mean a system by which a currency is convertible at a fixed exchange rate with another currency. This can mean that the currency is fully backed by a hard currency. Hard currency, in economic terms, refers to a currency in which investors have confidence. That is, currency from a politically stable country with low inflation and consistent monetary and fiscal policies. In particular, a currency that is tending to appreciate against other currencies on a trade-weighted basis. Examples of hard currencies include the United States dollar, the euro, the pound sterling, the Japanese yen, and the Swiss franc. The Deutschmark was considered the best hard currency until it was replaced by the euro. Today, many countries set their currency against a 'basket' of currencies. This basket of currencies is usually based on those of their trading partners, which are 'weighted' and measured to provide an average. Does that answer your question? Good.

Unit 1, Lesson 4, Exercise D 🎧 1.10

Lecture 5

Computers are also used for an electronic funds transfer (EFT). This includes transferring money from and to different bank accounts and for withdrawals. Most of us encounter EFT in our daily lives without thinking about it. For example, using an EFTPOS card as a customer to pay for goods in a shop or supermarket. EFTPOS stands for electronic funds transfer at point of sale.

The procedure works like this. A customer buys some goods at a supermarket. The customer takes the goods to the checkout, where the value is entered onto an electronic point of sale terminal (EPOS). The customer presents his or her EFTPOS card instead of cash. The EFTPOS card debits the customer's account and credits the retailer's account electronically. The customer and retailer accounts are updated after the transactions are uploaded on the computer. They are processed overnight.

Another example of an automated procedure is automated teller machines, or ATMs. ATMs allow bank clients access to their accounts 24 hours a day, seven days a week. This access is also possible in foreign countries. Bank clients are provided with an ATM card.

The bank client inserts the card into the machine. The machine asks for the personal identification number or PIN. The client then keys in their electronic code. The machine checks the code and, if it recognizes it, asks which transaction the client wants to make. The client can now withdraw money, check balances or, in some cases, transfer or deposit money. The most frequent transaction is the withdrawal, in which case the customer keys in the amount and the ATM checks if there are sufficient funds available in the client's account. If so, the machine returns the card and then pays the money, or pays the money and then returns the card. The order is different in some countries.

Unit 3, Lesson 2, Exercise B 🎧 1.11

Part 1

OK. Is everybody here? Right, let's start.

In the first lecture, I mentioned that banks are part of the larger financial services industry. You will remember that banks, as a licensed institution, are a distinct category of financial institution. Today, we'll be looking at different types of banking institutions. We'll start by looking at the question of ownership, before looking in greater detail at the types of services offered by different institutions.

Banking institutions may be defined by their ownership. For example, commercial banks – joint stock banks – are owned by share (or stock) holders, who are either private investors or bank holding companies. The term commercial bank is used to distinguish it from an investment bank. Commercial banks provide loans to businesses. They also accept and manage deposits for businesses and individuals, and provide mortgage finance and loans. They aim to make a profit, which is paid out in the form of dividends to their shareholders, though sometimes it's retained to build capital or net worth.

Building societies are included here (or SLAs - that is, savings and loan associations in the US and Canada). They specialize in providing mortgage finance and deposit and savings accounts. Some building societies or SLAs are mutuals, or mutual savings banks. These are owned by depositors – that is, the people who put money into accounts in the bank – and run by an elected board of trustees. They're profit-orientated, but their objective is either to build capital, lower future loan rates or raise future deposit rates for deposit owners.

Credit unions, popular in Canada and the US, are cooperatives owned by their members. They don't operate for profit, but retain surplus funds to build capital. They provide their members with the

same services as the retail banks. Typically, their members work for the same employer, but they can also be based on residence in the same geographical area.

Unit 3, Lesson 2, Exercise C 🎧 1.12

Part 2

Other classifications of banking institutions are possible. In the first lecture I made a broad distinction between wholesale, retail and central (or government) banks. The distinction between retail and wholesale banks has to do with the services they provide. Wholesale banks focus mainly on business-to-business banking services. Their clients are the merchant banks, or investment banks as they are known in the US, and other financial institutions.

Building societies, savings and loans, savings and retail banks are sometimes called depository (or deposit-taking) institutions. Retail banks provide individual services for the mass market. These include savings and cheque accounts, mortgages, personal loans, debit and credit cards, and so on. There is nothing inherently different about savings banks. In the UK some savings banks offer online services only. Savings and loan associations or credit unions are sometimes referred to as thrift banks in the US.

However, even if they're non-profit operations, banks need to cover their costs. And there are a variety of ways in which banks make money. The most common methods, as you know, are that they charge interest on loans. They finance these loans with their deposits. Although depositors earn interest on their money, it is re-lent by the bank at a higher rate. Banks operate on fractionalized deposits: that is, only a fraction of the total deposits in the bank is required, by law, to be kept in reserve. Banks also borrow money – for example, from other financial institutions – at a discount rate, and recycle it for better returns. Finally, banks charge fees for their services: cheque fees, ATM fees, and so on.

Unit 3, Lesson 2, Exercise D 🎧 1.13

Part 3

An institution can be defined as an organization that is both large and important. A web search for the top banking institutions is dominated by the Wall Street investment banks, the large American banks. These merchant banks, as they are known in the UK, operate for profit ... big profit! In terms of banking, the merchant or investment banks are perceived as extremely important, and capable of generating huge profits (or indeed losses). Sometimes referred to as money market or money centre banks, they have a global presence, and their knowledge of international finance makes them the specialists in dealing with multinational corporations.

In the UK, merchant banks traditionally provide finance to companies to enable them to increase the share capital of their subsidiary companies. They act as an intermediary between an issuer of securities and the investing public, they facilitate mergers and corporate reorganizations, and act as a broker for institutional clients. In the US, corporate banking, brokering, or underwriting private local US banks are part of their services.

When a company decides to go public and sell stock, investment banks underwrite IPOs – initial public offerings. They also fund LBOs. This term, leveraged buyout, refers to the takeover of a company whereby the company assets are the security for the money lent by the bank.

The traditional trading banks have a very conservative image. They loan money and make investments to businesses to buy, sell and merge. However, the merchant or investment banks are very entrepreneurial. For example, they have moved into areas traditionally dominated by insurance companies and share brokers. In fact, merchant or investment banking may not even be the largest part of their revenue stream. For some, that may now be their retail or insurance services, although asset management is still an important sector.

Unit 3, Lesson 2, Exercise E 🎧 1.14

Part 4

So, to summarize, banking institutions can be defined according to their ownership, or by the services they offer.

If they're defined by ownership, they fall into two basic categories: those owned by their members, such as cooperatives and building societies, and those owned by shareholders, or stock holders as they're called in the US. Cooperatives aim to build capital and improve interest rates for their members. Banks owned by shareholders operate for profit which is paid in the form of dividends to the shareholders.

If they're defined by their services, they can be broadly categorized into three major groups. These are wholesale banks, offering corporate banking, brokering or underwriting services; retail banks, providing services for the mass market; and central or government banks.

The term commercial is used to make a distinction between a commercial and an investment bank, which focuses on capital markets and large multinational corporations. However, since these two genres no longer have to be separate organizations, the term commercial bank is often used to refer to bank activities which focus mainly on companies. Investment banks include the multinational conglomerates whose subsidiary companies all provide very different banking products and services. For example, one American conglomerate, Citigroup, is involved in commercial and retail lending, owns a merchant bank, an investment bank and a private bank. It also has subsidiaries which offer offshore banking services.

Finally, whatever the type of institution, all banks must cover their operating costs or else they will fail over time.

OK, that's it for today. Next time we'll do a brief survey of the services offered by some of the banks operating in the UK. Don't forget to do a bit of research on that before you come. Thank you.

Unit 3, Lesson 2, Exercise F 🎧 1.15

1 Building societies are a type of investment bank.
2 Cooperatives are a type of banking institution owned by different banking groups.
3 By law, banks are required to keep in reserve only a fraction of their total deposits.
4 Investment banks are not profit-orientated.
5 Banks are never entrepreneurial.
6 In the past, banks were not involved in insurance or share market services.

Unit 3, Lesson 3, Exercise A 🎧 1.16

1 'dividends
2 'capital
3 in'surance
4 sub'sidiaries

5 in'vestors

6 'profitable

7 con'glomerate

8 'broking

9 'management

10 'leveraged

11 inte'gration

12 'mortgages

13 com'mission

Unit 3, Lesson 4, Exercise B 🎧 1.17

Part 1

In the last lecture we talked about banking institutions. We categorized them by their ownership and the services they offer. I mentioned that the large banking institutions engage in multiple activities and gave, as an example, one of the American conglomerates. Since we have time, I thought it might be useful to check out some of the websites of banks that operate in Britain and see what services they offer. Let's look first at the bank that promotes itself as the world's leading direct savings bank, ING Direct. What services do you think they offer? … You're right; they're mainly a savings bank. You can open an account with them over the telephone and access your accounts with them online. They also offer home insurance.

How do the services offered by the Alliance and Leicester, a commercial bank, differ? Well, to start with, this was previously a building society. That should give you a clue. I said at the start that building societies are included in the commercial bank category, and they specialize in providing mortgage finance, as well as deposit and savings accounts. As a visit to their website reveals, the Alliance and Leicester has a retail banking site providing current accounts, loans, mortgages, savings and credit card services, and a commercial banking site with services including money transmission, financing and investing. Next I'll discuss Barclays Bank.

Unit 3, Lesson 4, Exercise C 🎧 1.18

Part 2

Barclays promotes itself as a global financial service provider. In other words, it's another conglomerate. Its UK services include current accounts, savings and investments, loans, mortgages, insurance and credit cards. It offers both personal and business banking.

HSBC is one of the largest banking conglomerates and its shares are listed in the FTSE 100 in London. It has personal, business and corporate divisions and provides services including current accounts, savings and investments, finance, payments, credit cards, loans, mortgages, insurance, and international services. Its corporate division includes corporate and institutional, global markets payments and cash management, private equity, securities and trade services.

Unit 3, Lesson 4, Exercise D 🎧 1.19

Part 3

Finally, a brief look at two very different banks: first direct Internet savings bank, and the Islamic Bank of Britain. We'll start with first direct. As you can see, it offers a variety of services, from current and savings accounts, mortgages, loans, insurance, credit cards, to text message banking and touch-screen share dealing via the Internet.

The Islamic Bank of Britain provides retail banking services to individuals and small businesses in accordance with Islamic shariah principles. The personal services it provides include current accounts plus savings and home-buying accounts.

Unit 3, Lesson 4, Exercise F 🎧 1.20

Part 4

Well, I think that what this exercise has confirmed for us is … is that today, it is the integrated bank model that prevails. As we have seen, banking institutions engage in multiple activities and will, I think, continue to diversify in the future.

Unit 5, Lesson 2, Exercise B 🎧 1.21

Part 1

Good morning, everyone. To start with, I'm going to talk about how we can assess the financial strength of a bank. What do we mean by 'strength'? How do we measure this?

Well, we can look at a comparative analysis; that is, how the particular bank compares with other banks, or how it compares with its own performance in previous years. In this lecture I'm going to focus on individual bank performance and ... the bank we will be looking at is the ANW Bank. I'll use the financial accounts in the shareholders' report, which contains two tables of interest to us. These are the statement of financial performance, and the statement of financial position. While both these documents provide different information on the bank's financial strength, the statement of financial position is arguably the document for understanding the state of the bank's finances.

The main discussion will be on the statement of financial position. Firstly, I'll define exactly what a statement of financial position is. Then I'll briefly go over the categories included in a statement of financial position. I'll start with assets, followed by liabilities. After that, I'll look at equity.

Finally, I'll talk briefly about the statement of financial performance. This shows the movements in income, expenditure and profit which have taken place since the end of the previous accounting period. In other words, it shows the trading results for 12 months.

Unit 5, Lesson 2, Exercise E 🎧 1.22

Part 2

A statement of financial position shows what the bank has in the categories of assets, liabilities and equity at a certain date. In other words, the book value of the bank at a certain point in time. Before we look at the figures, I'll briefly go over what each of these categories includes.

The basic equation is that what the company owns, including money owed to the bank, must equal what the bank owes to its creditors and shareholders. In other words, assets must balance with liabilities and capital. Capital, of course, is not an asset. It is owed to the shareholders and would be paid back to them if the bank closed down.

If you look at the handout, you will see that the bank's assets are made up, firstly, of 'Cash and liquid assets' – that is, for example, cheques in the process of collection, and demand securities. In other words, those assets that can readily be turned into cash.

Next we have 'Due from other financial institutions', which includes advances and loans made by the ANW Bank to other banks. This is not to be confused with 'Due to other financial institutions', which forms part of the bank's liabilities and includes advances and loans made to the ANW Bank by other banks.

Continuing with assets, we have 'Trading securities', which include negotiable financial instruments. Negotiable financial instruments are basically financial instruments that can be assigned to another purchaser at any time. What I mean is, for example, government bonds purchased by the bank.

Financial instruments held for the long term are included under 'Investments and securities'. Arguably, they could be included in a financial instruments category. It follows that the bank's shares in listed companies are included under 'Investments and securities'.

Actually, the largest type of assets held by a bank is normally loans and advances made to bank customers, which is the next category.

And finally, we have the fixed assets held by the bank. These are fundamentally the 'Property, plant and equipment' owned by the bank.

Unit 5, Lesson 2, Exercise F 🎧 1.23

Part 3

The largest group of liabilities is generally 'Deposits and other borrowings'. These represent deposits and other advances made by bank customers. 'Income tax liabilities' – well, that's pretty self-explanatory – and ... 'Bonds and notes' – which are financial instruments issued by the bank to raise funds to lend to customers.

Now if you look at the handout, you'll see that in this example the date, March 31st, 2007, is preceded by the words 'as at'. It shows the financial strength of the organization on that particular day. In our example, the statement of financial position presents a view of the ANW Bank's financial position at two points of time. The figures are presented for March 31st, 2007 with comparative figures for the same date in the previous year, that is, 2006.

The words 'for the year ended ...' refer to the date which is the end of the financial year for an organization. In other words, its annual balance date. This is not to be confused with the end of the calendar year. Year end balance dates are commonly December 31st, March 31st, or June 30th, subject to the tax regime of the country concerned. The reporting format may vary between banks ... and also by country. While there are international accounting standards, each country can modify these for their own particular legal requirements ... um ... where was I? Oh yes, to return to the main point, a country could have quarterly, or six-monthly or annual reporting requirements.

And now … to go back to liabilities. Naturally, banks have to make financial provisions to provide for potential losses, such as, for example, the non-repayment of loans made to customers. 'Provisions' includes the provision made for future risk, whereas 'subordinated debt' includes loans to the bank that have a lower level of security. The 'Provisions' category is basically the financial allowances made by the bank to provide for potential losses and is necessary in order to give a true and fair view of the bank's financial position.

Unit 5, Lesson 3, Exercise B 🎧 1.24

Part 4

Now, if you look at the figures for 'Net assets' in the handout, you will see that they are the difference between total assets and total liabilities. Net assets must equal total equity.

'Equity' represents the shareholders' financial interest in the bank. In our example it is made up of 'Contributed equity', 'Reserves' and 'Retained profits'. 'Contributed equity' is the amount of capital contributed by the shareholders. 'Reserves' include the surplus generated from revaluing assets or from selling assets. 'Retained profits' are the accumulated annual profits that remain after paying income tax and dividends to shareholders.

As I said, the total equity amount must equal net assets. The bank's equity should remain positive and preferably growing. The bank regulator can close a bank if its equity gets too low relative to its total assets. Now, the point about this is … Oh, I see we're running out of time. Before I see you next time, I'd like you all to do some research. The topic is 'capital to asset ratio'. We'll discuss what you've found next time I see you.

Unit 5, Lesson 3, Exercise C 🎧 1.25

1 com'parative
2 'generally
3 e'quation
4 con'tributed
5 se'curities
6 re'tained
7 'arguably

8 a'ccumulated
9 re'gime
10 pre'ceded
11 'equity
12 a'nalysis

Unit 5, Lesson 3, Exercise D 🎧 1.26

Negotiable financial instruments are basically financial instruments that can be assigned to another purchaser at any time. What I mean is, for example, government bonds purchased by the bank.

Financial instruments held for the long term are included under 'Investments and securities'. Arguably, they could be included in a financial instruments category. It follows that the bank's shares in listed companies are included under 'Investments and securities'.

Actually, the largest type of assets held by a bank is normally loans and advances made to bank customers, which is the next category.

And finally, we have the fixed assets held by the bank. These are fundamentally the 'Property, plant and equipment' owned by the bank.

Unit 5, Lesson 4, Exercise B 🎧 1.27

Extract 1

LECTURER: Right, Liz and Amy, what did you find out about capital to asset ratio?

AMY: Well, the banking regulations in most countries require banks to have a capital adequacy ratio.

LIZ: It's the capital to asset ratio we were supposed to research!

Extract 2

LECTURER: Both terms are correct. What do they mean?

AMY: They refer to the amount of money a bank has to have in the form of shareholders' capital. It's 8% of the bank's assets.

LIZ: I'm not sure it's a straightforward calculation. The assets are weighted according to their risk.

PAUL: Well, I read that the Bank for International Settlements, which most countries belong to, has set a guideline for a minimum capital adequacy ratio of 8%.

MARK: Isn't the Bank for International Settlements based in Switzerland?

Extract 3

LECTURER: OK, if we look at the figures in our example, how does the ANW Bank measure up? Paul, what about you?

PAUL: Sorry, I don't really know.

Extract 4

LECTURER: Liz, what do you have to say about the capital ratio for the ANW Bank?

LIZ: Well, their assets for 2007 are $231,515,000.

PAUL: And total equity is only $16,910,000.

Extract 5

LECTURER: Paul, can you explain the relevance of the total equity figure?

PAUL: Well, total equity as a percentage of total assets gives us the capital adequacy ratio. In the example, this is less than the guideline set by the Bank for International Settlements of …

AMY: Actually, it's 7.3%.

Unit 5, Lesson 4, Exercise C 🎧 1.28

Extract 6

LECTURER: Let's go back to the handout for the moment to see how it can help explain capital ratio. First of all, tell us what you understand by this term.

AMY: Well, in our research we found two terminologies. They mean the same thing, don't they, Liz?

LIZ: Absolutely. The terms used were 'capital to asset ratio' and 'capital adequacy ratio'.

Extract 7

AMY: They refer to the amount of money a bank has to have in the form of shareholders' capital. The Bank for International Settlements, which most countries belong to, has set a guideline for a minimum capital adequacy ratio of 8%.

MARK: Sorry, I don't follow. Could you explain why it's important?

PAUL: Well, basically, it's to protect the depositors in the event of a run on the bank's money.

AMY: Yes, it's a way of ensuring that, in a bank crisis, the shareholders have some cash available to repay the depositors.

Extract 8

MARK: I don't understand how to find this ratio in our handout.

LIZ: Well, one method is to work out what percentage total equity is of total assets. For instance, in 2007 their assets are $231,515,000 and total equity is $16,910,000.

Extract 9

LIZ: Yes, and the percentage we arrive at is 7.3%.

PAUL: If I understand you correctly, you're saying that it's below the recommended minimum.

LIZ: Yes, that's right.

Extract 10

LIZ: This is all very interesting, isn't it?

PAUL: Yes, it seems that the ANW Bank shareholders have not made adequate protection for their depositors in the event of a financial crisis in the banking industry.

AMY: Correct!

LECTURER: However, before we are too critical of the bank's shareholders – it's not a straightforward calculation. The assets are weighted according to their risk, and we don't have that information.

Unit 7, Lesson 2, Exercise B 🎧 1.29

Part 1

Good morning, everyone. What I'm going to talk about today is a core activity of international banking. That is, the financial and intermediary role international banks play in international trade. I will also introduce various payment terms, bearing in mind that these depend on many factors. As we know, the parties involved in international trade are not resident in the same country. Generally, the seller of the goods is the exporter, while another term for the buyer is importer.

Because banks are considered to be reliable as well as creditworthy, they facilitate international trade. They do this by adhering to universally accepted International Chamber of Commerce guidelines. These guidelines assist the exporters and importers by meeting their varying financing needs. Different financial instruments have been developed to meet different requirements. In other words, banks offer specialized financing products. Banks also facilitate finance for government-backed schemes. Today, however, we will deal with financing and payment methods.

Plus, of course, the security offered and terms of payment. This whole operational sequence is also known as international trade finance. What I mean is, it's everything involved in selecting the best option from a variety of financing and payment methods for a particular export transaction.

So, ... in later lectures, we'll also go on to consider the associated risks when determining payment options, and we'll be taking a look at international regulations.

Unit 7, Lesson 2, Exercise C 🎧 1.30

Part 2

As we have seen in an earlier session, international trade can be thought of as a process that starts with a buyer, or purchaser, of goods. In international trade, this person or company may also be known as the importer, and the seller may be referred to as the exporter.

Today we're going to look at some of the different payment terms or methods. As we saw previously, there are a number of payment options available. Today we will focus on four of these, including letter of credit, documentary collection, cash with order and cash on delivery. And then, finally, if there is time available, we will look at financing costs and the degree of risk involved for the importer, the exporter and the banks in the terms and transfer of payment.

Unit 7, Lesson 2, Exercise E 🎧 1.31

Part 3

Now, an important concept in selecting finance is the notion of an 'optimal' source of finance. What do I mean by 'optimal' source? Banks, when considering finance options and terms, take into consideration the stage or stages in the transaction at which finance is required. Finance is usually required by either or both of the parties at two distinct stages: either at the pre-shipment stage or the post-shipment stage. The bank also looks at who assumes responsibility for the goods at what stage in the transaction.

In financial terms, there is a direct relationship between the risks involved and the terms and costs of finance. Say, for example, the bank considers that there is a high risk for the exporter of payment default, then it would advise the exporter to try to obtain cash with the order. In this way, the exporter is provided with pre-shipment finance to process and ship the goods.

Another factor is the length of time finance is required – short, medium, or long-term. A letter of credit involves completing a lot of documentation and may be too costly when finance is required for a short period on a small order.

The difference between a letter of credit and documentary collection is that, although documentary collection may be less expensive, the banks don't guarantee payment. It is less secure but, looking at it another way, it could be the best option for both exporter and importer if they have an established trading relationship. As you can see, then, obtaining optimal payment terms involves many factors. The point is that no one method is going to be optimal for all companies and all situations.

Unit 7, Lesson 2, Exercise F 🎧 1.32

Part 4

Now ... let's see ... oh dear, I see we're running short of time ... but perhaps I should just say something about the basic mechanism of each of the four financing options mentioned.

The payment form most beneficial to the exporter is cash with order. With this type of payment, the importer pays for the goods pre-shipment. After the exporter's bank receives the payment, the exporter sends the documents, then ships the goods to the importer. The importer may need to raise short- to medium-term finance to cover the period between payment and receipt and sale of the goods. As the bank cannot take security over the goods, since ownership of them varies depending on the agreement, it usually takes a security in the form of a debenture over the assets of the importer's company.

A letter of credit is the most common form of payment used in international trade. In this situation, the importer raises the letter of credit at the request of the exporter. First the importer's bank issues a document stating a commitment to pay the seller, on behalf of the buyer, a specified amount under precisely defined conditions and on a specific date. This commitment is irrevocable. Then the exporter has to submit the title document to the goods, plus other documents, to the importer's bank. After the goods are shipped, provided the documents have been received, the importer's bank makes payment on the due date.

Documentary collection offers less security than a letter of credit. What happens here is the exporter's bank receives payment, or a bill of exchange, against the shipping documents. First, an exporter sends the title documents (including the bill of exchange) through its bank to the buyer's bank. After acceptance or payment of the bill of exchange by the importer, the exporter instructs the bank to release the goods to the importer. The importer has the right to take ownership of the shipment after obtaining the title documents.

Cash on delivery terms are used only when the exporter is confident that there is no risk involved. What's different to the previous options is that the exporter ships the goods and sends the commercial documents directly to the buyer. Only after satisfactory receipt of the goods by the importer does the exporter receive payment. This method offers the least security for the exporter, who is completely dependent on the buyer to make payment. Because the exporter is paid after delivery, and the exchange rate may have changed, the exporter may want to take a foreign exchange contract on the transaction. Under such an arrangement an agreed exchange rate is fixed so that the exporter is guaranteed a certain price even if exchange rates change.

Unit 7, Lesson 3, Exercise A 🎧 1.33

1 'optimal
2 depreci'ation
3 fi'nancial
4 de'cision
5 fluctu'ation
6 sig'nificant
7 con'tributing
8 cri'teria
9 ex'change
10 insta'bility
11 i'rrevocable
12 'merchandise

Unit 7, Lesson 3, Exercise B 🎧 1.34

Extract 1

The payment form most beneficial to the exporter is cash with order. With this type of payment, the importer pays for the goods pre-shipment. After the exporter's bank receives the payment, the exporter sends the documents, then ships the goods to the importer. The importer may need to raise short- to medium-term finance to cover the period between payment and receipt and sale of the goods. As the bank cannot take security over the goods, since ownership of them varies depending on the agreement, it usually takes a security in the form of a debenture over the assets of the importer's company.

Extract 2

Documentary collection offers less security than a letter of credit. What happens here is the exporter's bank receives payment, or a bill of exchange, against the shipping documents. First, an exporter sends the title documents (including the bill of exchange) through its bank to the buyer's bank. After acceptance or payment of the bill of exchange by the importer, the exporter instructs the bank to release the goods to the importer. The importer has the right to take ownership of the shipment after obtaining the title documents.

Unit 7, Lesson 3, Exercise D 🎧 1.35

Part 5

I'm going to finish with some comments on the main factors influencing the terms of payment. Now, the fact of the matter is, it's a highly complex task to decide on the optimal financing terms. Payment terms have to take into account a wide variety of different factors – not to mention the fact that some of these factors are totally outside the control of the company. The reason for this is that there is no method for predicting, for example, currency fluctuations, after the order has been placed. In other words, changes in the exchange rates between the countries. You've probably heard of the Asian currency crisis. It was in the late 1990s that there was a rapid depreciation of Asian currencies. It was Mohamad Mahathir, the Malaysian prime minister at the time, who placed restrictions on US dollar payments to all foreign organizations. All organizations trading with Malaysian companies had to accept payments in the Malaysian currency. You can imagine the consequences for foreign trading companies. Plus there's the fact that significant economic instability can lead to political instability. Let's take Indonesia as an example. It can be argued that the Asian financial crisis was a contributing factor in the overthrow of the Suharto government.

OK. Where was I ? Oh, yes … The advantage of having a variety of payment options is that some are more suited to a particular trading situation than others. Let me put it another way … in any decision regarding payment terms there are a number of criteria that have to be considered, including, for example, the risks involved, the size of the order and the nature of the merchandise; the distance between buyer and seller; etcetera.

Oh, I almost forgot to mention your research tasks. OK, well, I've briefly mentioned some of the factors influencing financing options. However, I'd like you to do some further research on this.

One important aspect is the relationship between the exporter and importer. Also, what's very important for the whole transaction is the size of the order and the component costs. So I'd also like you to find out the main criteria that need to be borne in mind by bankers when assisting a company to decide on financing options for various overseas trading ventures.

Unit 7, Lesson 4, Exercise C 🎧 1.36

Extract 1

Now, as we know, it is very important for companies to obtain optimal payment terms for their export orders. I asked you to look at the case of Rainbow Corporation, a Singapore personal computer manufacturer which has decided to significantly expand its export markets. Rainbow Corporation already has an export market in China. However, the company director has decided to double the volume of sales from 20,000 to 40,000 units per annum. The company has now taken orders from Indonesia, Belgium, New Zealand and Mexico. It has come to the bank to get advice on the optimal payment terms for financing the orders. I would like you to give your rationale for the terms you recommend in each situation.

Unit 7, Lesson 4, Exercise D 🎧 1.37

Extract 2

JACK: Well, I'll start with Indonesia. I'd like to make two points. First, I think there's a high risk of payment default on this order.

LEILA: Can you expand on that, Jack?

JACK: Sure, Leila. Indonesia is a country where the legal processes for recovery of payment are uncertain.

LEILA: So?

JACK: So the point is that in this case the exporter should ask for cash with the order.

LECTURER: OK. So, what's your second point, Jack?

JACK: I was coming to that! My second point is that this is an order from a private company operating only in Indonesia.

LEILA: Yes, but that's true for Mexico, too. Even more so, I'd say, as the Mexican order is from a new client. So I think the risk of default is higher.

MAJED: Well, I don't agree with that, Leila, because we don't know if the Indonesian client is new or not.

EVIE: Sorry, but what are we talking about, exactly? I think before we decide on the payment terms we need to take into account other factors such as the order size.

LEILA: Yes, we need to be clear here. I think payment terms must be based on a number of factors. I'd just like to say that according to what I've read, the Indonesian order is the best example of one where cash with order terms would be best.

EVIE: In what way?

LEILA: Well when you look at the size of the order, you'll see that it will require a large number of imported components, I mean the chips and so on, so this is the best method for financing the working capital required for the order.

MAJED: I don't understand why you don't recommend a letter of credit, because it's the most common method of financing international trade. How can you get an importer to pay for goods not yet manufactured? Can you give me an example, Leila?

LEILA: OK. Look at it this way. A letter of credit facility involves a lot of documentation and consequently extra costs in bank charges. If the importer has the funds, has confidence in the exporter and wants to secure the order with the minimum amount of administration, then cash with order terms probably seems like the best option. There may also be foreign exchange benefits.

JACK: I don't get that. Foreign exchange benefits for whom?

LEILA: For the importer. What I'm trying to say is that in this case, as Indonesia is more likely to be subject to currency fluctuations than Singapore, the importer might benefit from paying in advance for the order if the Indonesian currency is predicted to depreciate.

MAJED: So everybody wins! In this situation cash with order is the best option.

LECTURER: Absolutely. In making a decision on financing international trade, companies have to think about their fixed and variable costs, as well as the revenue they're likely to get from a particular order. OK, that's it for today. I'd like you to look at the best financing options for the Belgium, New Zealand and Mexico orders for next time. Make sure you consider all the options and can justify your choices.

Unit 9, Lesson 2, Exercise B 🎧 2.1

Part 1

Good morning, everyone. I'm going to talk to you this morning about banking in developing countries. However, before we can discuss the nature of their banking systems, we need to have an understanding of what we are referring to when we make the distinction between a developing country and other countries. Firstly, I'll identify the main terms used, then I'll briefly discuss the types of banking institution operating in developing countries.

Now to start with, there is no definitive classification nor is there an established convention for the designation of 'developing' countries or areas. As we shall see, it depends on the focus of the institution making the classification. Geographers tend to focus on development indicators. Investment information sources – for example, The Economist – or market index makers – for example, MSCI, Morgan Stanley Capital International – tend to focus on the level of economic development. MSCI makes the distinction between countries with developed markets, and those with emerging markets. The terms used may describe markets, regions or countries.

In terms of the so-called 'developed' countries, this generally includes the member countries of the OECD (that is, the Organisation for Economic Co-operation and Development, which replaced the Organisation for European Economic Co-operation in 1961). Their economies are referred to by the World Bank and the IMF respectively as 'high-income' and 'advanced' economies. However, given that anomalies exist in the terminology used when determining any country's classification, the World Bank 1997 classification of nations by income makes a good starting point.

OK, so let's take a few moments to think about this classification. From the point of view of the World Bank, the world's countries can be classified into five income-based categories: 1) high-income OECD members, for example, Japan, Canada, France; 2) high-income non-OECD economies, for example, United Arab Emirates, Hong Kong, Kuwait, Singapore; 3) upper middle-income economies, for example, Saudi Arabia, Argentina; 4) lower middle-income economies, for example, Turkey, Egypt; and 5) low-income economies, for example, Zimbabwe and Cambodia. As I mentioned earlier, both the terminology and the categorization of countries are continually changing, depending on the basis for the classification. Financial development and gross domestic product are often used as indicators. However, it's true to say that a major point of division can be identified between high-income countries, and the others.

So ... to get back to the World Bank classifications. To start with, the World Bank classification of 'low-income economies' approximates to countries that are also classified as less developed countries (LDCs) and highly indebted poor countries (HIPCs). But as we shall see, these tend to have a different emphasis – I'll come back to this in a little while and tell you some of the similarities and differences.

Low-income economies are generally equated with a poor infrastructure and an economy based on agriculture and natural resource extraction. A country is classified as LDC if it is characterized by low income, unskilled human resources, and a low level of economic diversification, that is, it is predominantly an agriculturally based subsistence economy. The term HIPC was formalized by the World Bank and the IMF in 1996. This designation was based on a value of debt service to gross domestic product exceeding 80%, or a value of debt to exports exceeding 220%.

Lower-middle-income economies, the next category, can be loosely included in the group referred to in other data as NICs (that is, newly industrialized countries) – although the categorization of NICs is an economic as opposed to an income-based category.

To summarize so far ... the definition of developing countries used in this lecture includes all the World Bank classifications except for the high-income categories (in other words, the high-income OECD members and the high-income economies). I think there are about 33 countries, that's approximately 18% of the world's countries, that fall into this high-income category. So it should be clear that what we're focusing on is the banking arrangements that exist for the other – approximately 82% – of the world's countries.

So, what sort of banking arrangements do we find in developing countries? It could be argued that banking structures in the developing countries are not that different from those of the high-income economies, with commercial banks providing about 90% of the total credit for everyday business activities. However, there are a number of international and regional institutions that provide financial support for economic development activities only in developing countries. These are the multilateral banks. As the term multilateral indicates, the membership of these banks may include other international banks and governments. Their contributions are pooled and then disbursed at the discretion of the agency.

Multilateral banks have been categorized by the World Bank into three major groups, based on their membership and mandate. The first group consists of international institutions, including the World Bank itself. They are large regional institutions known as the multilateral development banks (MDBs). This group includes the African Development Bank, the Asian Development Bank, the European Bank for Reconstruction and Development, and the Inter-American Development Bank.

The membership of these MDBs is not exclusively limited to member countries of the developing region, but also includes some high-income country government donors. For example, the UK Department for International Development is a shareholder and contributor to the African, Asian, and Inter-American development banks as well as the European Bank for Reconstruction and Development.

The second major group in the World Bank category are described as the multilateral financial institutions (MFIs). The distinction between MDBs and MFIs is that MFIs have a narrower membership structure and may focus on specific sectors or activities. Included in this category are the European Investment Bank, the Islamic Development Bank, the Nordic Investment Bank, plus organizations such as OPEC ... do you all know what that stands for? No? Well, it means the Organization of the Petroleum Exporting Countries ... As I was saying, MFIs also include the OPEC Fund for International Development, and the International Fund for Agricultural Development.

Thirdly, there is the group of institutions referred to as sub-regional banks. This group includes the Central American Bank for Economic Integration, the East African Development Bank, and the West African Development Bank.

While the majority of the multilateral banks focus on what I call macro-programmes – that is, large

loans that assist developing and aid-recipient countries – there is a fourth category of institutions that offer very small loans to populations ineligible for loans from traditional banks. They are the micro-finance institutions such as the Grameen Bank in Bangladesh. However, I will discuss multilateral banks and micro-finance institutions in more detail later ...

Unit 9, Lesson 2, Exercise C 🎧 2.2

1 It could be argued that banking structures in the developing countries are not that different from those of the high-income economies.

2 But as we shall see, these tend to have a different emphasis – I'll come back to this in a little while and tell you some of the similarities and differences.

3 From the point of view of the World Bank, the world's countries can be classified into five income-based categories.

4 However, it's true to say that a major point of division can be identified between high-income countries, and the others.

5 So it should be clear that what we're focusing on is the banking arrangements that exist for the other – approximately 82% – of the world's countries.

Unit 9, Lesson 2, Exercise D 🎧 2.3

Part 2

So, to get back to the topic ... let's look at the multilateral banks in more detail. Firstly, the multilateral development banks ... The financial support, provided by the World Bank and other MDBs, for investment in economic development activities in developing countries, happens in distinct ways – although these different ways are also connected.

Firstly, there are the long-term loans, with interest based on market rates. Because of the size of multilateral development banks (remember: they include more than two groups or countries), they are able to borrow on international capital markets to fund these loans. They then re-lend this money to borrowing programmes in developing countries. Secondly, there are the very long-term loans, with concessional rates, that is, interest well below market rates. These very long-term loans are referred to as 'credits' and are funded through direct contributions from governments in donor countries. A third form of financial support is grant financing. This financing is provided by some MDBs for technical and advisory services or project preparation. The investments, for example, of the European Bank for Reconstruction and Development – which was established when communism was collapsing in Central and Eastern Europe – mainly involve taking equity in private enterprises with commercial partners. But the bank is also able to mobilize domestic capital, due to its size and credibility.

The World Bank has its criteria of minimum credit requirements for the businesses or government agencies seeking a loan. The ability to repay is one of the criteria for receiving a loan. That is, they must be creditworthy. However, within the World Bank there are two institutions providing financial assistance to separate developing country sectors.

The International Bank for Reconstruction and Development (IBRD) focuses on middle-income and creditworthy poor countries, whereas the International Development Association focuses on countries such as HIPCs (heavily indebted poor countries), which are ineligible for World Bank concessional, or below market rate, borrowing.

As I stated earlier, the multinational financial institutions have a narrower membership structure and may focus on specific sectors or activities. Let's focus on one example – the European Investment Bank. You don't need to take notes on this … Contrary to its name, the European Investment Bank, set up in 1958 by the Treaty of Rome, is not an investment bank. As a non-profit organization the EIB does not receive money from savings or current accounts. Nor does it receive funds from the European Union's budget – though the member states of the European Union do make contributions based on their economic position within the Union. Instead, the EIB is financed through borrowing on the financial markets. Bearing in mind that it has the backing of the European Union member states, you can understand that the EIB, like MDBs, can borrow very large amounts of capital on the world financial markets, at – I might add – very competitive terms. So its size and credibility enable the EIB to obtain loans which it in turn invests in projects that benefit the most disadvantaged regions. Generally, these projects would otherwise not get money – or would have to borrow it more expensively.

Let's move on now, to another MFI – the Islamic Development Bank (or IDB), which was formally opened in October 1975. Its purpose is to encourage economic and social development of member countries and Muslim communities. The bank is authorized to accept deposits and to mobilize financial resources. Members contribute to the bank's capital, which allows it to participate in equity capital and grant loans for productive projects and enterprises, as well as assisting Muslim communities in non-member countries.

The IDB follows the principles of shariah, or Islamic jurisprudence. By the way, does anyone know what shariah-compatible practices include? Well, they aim to follow the principles of the Qur'an, which in the common non-Islamic perspective are reflected in a prohibition of usury and the charging of interest. However, this is only one aspect of Islamic banking – we will look at this, and the other aspects, in more detail some other time.

Now, where was I? Oh, yes, I was talking about the multilateral finance institutions. If we turn now to the third group – the sub-regional banks. Sub-regional, of course, means the same as intra-regional; in other words, we are talking about a smaller part of a larger whole. The sub-regional banks differ from the other two categories in the following ways. The first significant difference is that they are typically owned by the borrowing members that make up their sub region. And the second major difference is that their focus is much more on poverty, infrastructure, and other key regional issues.

Finally, I would like to discuss a fourth category of institution. Whereas the previous three groups are all categorized as multilateral banks, this fourth category of institution exists in low-income economies in developing countries. Micro-credit projects provide very poor populations with loans for work schemes such as small weaving, irrigation or fishing projects to promote their economic self-development. In addition to loans, some micro-credit, or 'village banking' projects provide savings and other banking services.

So, what exactly have we looked at this morning? Well, to sum up, we need to understand the major differences between the multilateral institutions. Firstly, whereas multilateral development banks tend to look at large long-term loans to developing countries worldwide, multinational financial institutions tend to focus on specific activities or sectors. Sub-regional banks, on the other hand, are much more concerned with regional issues, including infrastructure and poverty. Furthermore, sub-regional banks are typically owned by the borrowing members of their sub region. In addition to the multilateral organizations, which operate at the macro level, there are the micro-credit institutions which provide loans for very poor populations ineligible for traditional banking services.

Unit 9, Lesson 3, Exercise A 🎧 2.4

1 'infrastructure, 'nationalized, fi'nancial, merger

2 'income based, 'banking structures, 'member countries, developing 'region.

3 'markets, 'regions, e'conomies, 'countries

4 inter'national insti'tutions, multilateral 'banks, emerging 'markets, competitive 'terms

Unit 9, Lesson 3, Exercise C 🎧 2.5

Part 3

OK, so moving on to look at banking structures in developing countries … to start with, I'd like to take a few moments to discuss the ownership of commercial banks.

The banking crisis in the 1980s and 1990s left many banking systems of emerging countries broken up. As Heffernan points out in Modern Banking (one of your core texts – the paperback edition was published in 2005) 126 banking crises were identified in developing market countries during this period. Consequently, during 1999 to 2004, there was a trend for bank consolidation, with the frequent occurrence of mergers, acquisitions and liquidations. In fact, mergers and acquisitions were seen by officials as a means of enlarging domestic banks, to make them more competitive with foreign banks … and a further important point, they were also a means of eliminating weak banks.

A study by the Bank for International Settlements showed that during the same period, across a number of developing country regions, the percentage of state-owned commercial banks declined, as governments in developing countries were motivated to sell government-owned institutions to skilled investors.

Let's look in a bit more detail at some specific regions, beginning with Latin America. Here, private domestic bank ownership declined from 79% in 1994 to 47% in 2004, while, over the same period, foreign-owned banks increased from 6% in 1994 to 42% in 2004. There was a similar trend in Central Europe over the same period.

By the way, I see that some of you are using the Cornell note-taking system. That's very good. Do you all know about this? No? Right, well, if you want to know more about it, I suggest you look at How to Study in College by Walter Pauk, P-A-U-K, the 8th edition, published in 2004. It's very good, and it should be in the University Library.

So to get back to the main topic … Over the last decade, the growth of globalization, trade, and financial integration have led to an increase in the number of foreign banks entering developing country regions via foreign direct investment (or FDI). A definition of foreign direct investment given in thefreedictionary.com on the Web is: 'long-term investment by a foreign direct investor in an enterprise resident in an economy other than that in which the foreign investor is based.'

The Multilateral Investment Guarantee Agency – which is part of the World Bank Group – was established to promote FDI by working with host governments in developing countries and investors in source countries. The agency provides guarantees to protect cross-border investment in developing member countries and also guarantees to protect investors. Mergers and acquisitions – including acquisitions involving the privatization of state enterprises – are a significant form of FDI.

There has been a large body of literature addressing the benefits and costs of privatization and foreign ownership of banks in developing countries. And there seems to be a consensus that foreign-bank participation generally increases competition, and makes the domestic banks more efficient – though it may affect their profitability. As Heffernan states: 'The foreign firm can bring in expertise and also train and educate the host country labour force …'; however, the extent to which FDI is beneficial to the host country also depends on the type of FDI.

While the majority of FDI is from high-income countries, there is also a trend for banks in developing countries to enter another developing country. One study found that 27% of all foreign banks in developing countries were owned by a bank from another developing country.

Developing-country foreign banks tend to operate intra-regionally and in developing countries that are unattractive to high-income country banks – on account of their small size, low income, and weak institutions. Although the source developing-country banks are not significant in terms of their assets (generally, they represent approximately 5% of foreign-bank assets in the host country), there is concern that they are disproportionately represented in low-income countries.

Certain characteristics in a particular host developing country may attract some source countries more than others. One obvious characteristic, for example, is that they share a common language. Whether the source is a high-income or another developing country, a common language reduces the cost of foreign direct banking for the source country. Other factors include a similar legal system, being in close proximity to each other, and economic integration.

Now, I think that's all I'm going to say for the moment on this topic. Are there any questions so far? No, good. As I said earlier, banking practices in developing countries and those in developed nations are similar, that is, commercial banks accept deposits and make loans. Banks may also finance government expenditure. However, many developing countries have common problems relating to their banking structure. For example, high operating costs (related to interest-rate ceilings), high inflation, and little competition. Now, when I see you in tutorials we'll look in more detail at some of the problems associated with banking in developing countries. In the meantime, I'm going to set you a research task. Right, now listen carefully … I'd like you to work in groups of three or four. I want you to research three types of commercial bank ownership in developing countries … each group will focus on only one type of ownership. Because the ownership criteria vary between countries, I want you to select two developing countries and compare the ownership rule defining the type of bank which you have chosen – namely private domestic, foreign-owned, or state-owned.

Unit 9, Lesson 3, Exercise D 🎧 2.6

Extract 1

The banking crisis in the 1980s and 1990s left many banking systems of emerging countries fragmented. As Heffernan points out in Modern Banking (one of your core texts – the paperback edition was published in 2005) 126 banking crises were identified in developing market countries during this period.

Extract 2

By the way, I see that some of you are using the Cornell note-taking system. That's very good. Do you all know about this? No? Right, well, if you want to know more about it, I suggest you look at How to Study in College by Walter Pauk, P-A-U-K, the 8th edition, published in 2004. It's very good, and it should be in the University Library.

Extract 3

One study found a correlation between the degree of bilateral trade between two countries and the occurrence of foreign direct investment from source to host country. A definition of foreign direct investment (FDI) given in thefreedictionary.com on the web is: 'long-term investment by a foreign direct investor in an enterprise resident in an economy other than that in which the foreign investor is based.'

Extract 4

There has been a large body of literature addressing the benefits and costs of privatization and foreign ownership of banks in developing countries. And there seems to be a consensus that foreign-bank participation generally increases competition, and makes the domestic banks more efficient – though it may affect their profitability. As Heffernan states: 'The foreign firm can bring in expertise and also train and educate the host country labour force …'; however, the extent to which FDI is beneficial to the host country also depends on the type of FDI.

Unit 9, Lesson 4, Exercise C 🎧 2.7

Extract 1

I think that the banking system in developing countries is characterized by their economic system. For example, a system of private enterprise banking characterizes capitalist countries, a nationalized banking system characterizes socialist countries. In Eastern Europe, for example, the newly privatized banks had problems relating to the overhanging debt from what were previously state-owned or nationalized institutions. They also had overly complicated organization structures, lack of accountability, and poor training of staff and management. Bank networks were more labour intensive … for example, more tellers but few or no ATMs. Electronic or Internet banking in developing countries is not extensive. Cash on delivery is still the preferred payment method for goods, and, for online orders, cash deposits into the bank account of the vendor. This not only reflects a resistance by the population to electronic payment methods, but also a lack of facilities in the banking system, such as automated clearing houses …

Extract 2

er ... I think one big difference between banking in developing countries and banking in high-income economies is the cost of banking in emerging economies ... it may be very high, for a variety of reasons. The government may be unstable, the country may have a reputation for nationalizing foreign firms, or there may be the threat of a government coup d'etat, also ... high interest-rate ceilings, high reserve requirements are necessary to attract customers ... So let's look at the chart and ... oh sorry, that's the wrong chart, just a minute ... right, so here is a chart showing some different reserve requirements for different countries ... er, you can see, I think, this difference ... do you have any questions about this chart?

Extract 3

Many developing countries have common problems relating to their banking structure. For example, high operating costs (related to interest-rate ceilings), high inflation, and little competition. Higher reserve requirements than those in high-income countries have also contributed to higher operating costs. There may be low pay scales, political interference in the management and regulatory systems of the financial sectors, with associated problems such as improper lending practices. The economies of many developing countries are cash-based because of the benefits cash offers for tax evasion, anonymity, and security. For example, where credit cards are used in these societies, every transaction may require 'explicit consent' (that is, a signature) from the card holder.

Extract 4

All business, including banking, in a foreign country always involves risk ... um... which is attributed to many issues. Take political stability or instability, for example ... in some countries, governments can change overnight ... next day it's a whole new ball game. I think we all agree that interest-rate ceilings and high reserve requirements tend to raise bank operating costs. Also economic factors like ... you know, the country's GDP and GNP. Inflation rates vary widely among developing countries ... in some countries it's sky high due to the economy growing too quickly. There are also the risks of operating within a developing country, for example security risk, operational risk, et cetera. Also, from the point of view of the host countries, failure of a foreign bank on their soil ... as you can imagine ... could have serious repercussions for their own banking industry.

Unit 11, Lesson 2, Exercise B 🎧 2.8

Part 1

Good morning. Today I'm going to focus on banking standards. That is to say, I shall be looking at some of the factors which may affect, or compromise, the way banks operate in their day-to-day banking, including some of the fraudulent behaviour banks have to deal with. Don't misunderstand me, I don't want to imply that banks, or their employees, commonly engage in fraudulent behaviour, but as we all know, banking scandals and crises are not uncommon.

To some degree, all banks today need to be aware of how their actions, anywhere in the world, affect and are perceived by their customers. It is fair to say that as a result of technological advances banking operations are more complex. Not only that, but globalization means banks need to be aware of the government policies of the country or countries with whom they operate. For example, how does a bank enforce compliance on a subsidiary in another jurisdiction? Should a bank handle funds from a country with dubious business practices when the origin of the funds is unclear? These questions and many more demonstrate the complexity of situations banks face. So, in an attempt to keep this discussion of banking standards and responsibilities reasonably simple, I'm going to summarize a few of the more interesting problems banks may be exposed to, and will conclude briefly with the policies and procedures required for maintaining standards in the industry.

Unit 11, Lesson 2, Exercise C 🎧 2.9

Part 2

To start with, let's look at technological factors. Banking is an information-based industry involved in the collection and use of a wide variety of its clients' personal information, including bank account numbers and bank balances. Moreover, banks hold information on their clients' creditworthiness and banking history – for example, whether they have been issued with credit, debit or smart cards.

While information technology has revolutionized banking operations (increasing efficiency and providing new products and services, such as Internet banking), it has compromised bank security.

Computer hacking has become widespread and increasingly more sophisticated to the extent that Internet fraud, through phishing, pharming, and spyware, is now a major area of concern for banks. The process known as 'spear phishing' is a case in point. The bank customer may receive a personalized e-mail purporting to come from the bank, which tricks the account holder into divulging their online banking password and other personal and financial information. In other scams, such as Trojan horse or keylogger, spyware is planted onto personal computers to steal personal identity numbers and financial account credentials. In the case of pharming, the computer user is directed to fraudulent websites via proxy servers, even though the URL seen on the browser appears to be correct. (For those of you unfamiliar with these terms, webopedia.com gives a good description.)

It's quite clear that privacy and data protection continue to be significant issues for financial institutions. Because of the risks of fraud, many customers choose to only view their accounts online and refrain from carrying out online banking transactions. This is a problem for the banks, however, who want to encourage greater use of Internet banking.

This means ultimately that the onus is on the banks to provide protection against Internet fraud. Client education programmes can, to some degree, raise customers' awareness of new forms of fraud, and of the need to notify their bank, as soon as they receive suspect e-mails. However, what banks really need is staff with the technical expertise to ensure that Internet access to their services is safe.

There is no doubt that fraud is a global concern. In 2005 Unisys conducted a survey into the increasing prevalence of online identity theft. At that time, 17% of US and 11% of UK consumers reported being a victim. In 2006 a Gartner Research survey found a 50% increase in ID theft victims compared to 2003. All the evidence shows that, as the acceptance of financial products such as credit cards grows, the risk of ID fraud also increases. What seems obvious is that banks (and their customers) have a responsibility for remaining vigilant and up to date with online security measures in order to protect themselves from Internet hackers.

Some people claim that biometric data, such as iris scans and fingerprints, could provide the

answer. However, it could be argued that this will not solve the problem, as the usefulness of biometrics depends on the quality (and therefore the cost) of the machine and the technology used. Other people favour 'two-factor identification'. In addition to a password, confirmation by cellphone is required. Two-factor identification puts another step in the way of criminals. Meanwhile, the US Department of Justice is updating and improving current federal laws so that identity thieves are appropriately penalized for using malicious spyware and keyloggers; and so that threats to steal or corrupt data on a victim's computer become illegal.

So far, we have been discussing behaviour external to the banks. However, problems can also arise within banks.

Economic factors, such as the current trend of diversification within banking, have encouraged banks into non-traditional activities, like bancassurance and other fee-related business, and can lead to possible conflicts of interest. Within the banking industry, as Heffernan (2004, p.21) points out, 'conflict-of-interest issues continue to surface. Banks are accused of fraud for inflating prices on stock firms and initial public offerings (IPOs).'

Problems may also occur on an international scale. In this information age, new technology has extended the global 'reach' of many businesses. Consequently, events in one country impinge on others. For example, in 2007 a 'sub-prime' mortgage crisis, originating in the United States, affected global financial markets. American mortgage agents had received financial incentives to sell mortgages. As a result, vast numbers of mortgage loans were sold to low-income families with no assessment of their credit risk. The American banks sold these loans on to large investment banks who packaged these debts into bonds, sold largely to foreign investors. The originating banks were not overly concerned about the borrower's ability to repay because they were intending to sell the loans. Rising defaults by sub-prime American mortgage borrowers resulted in banks becoming nervous about getting their money back and being unwilling to lend to one another. In the US, Europe, Japan and England, central banks, as lenders of the last resort, provided short-term funds to banks with insufficient liquidity.

It's quite clear that ethical questions need to be addressed regarding the originating banks' relaxation of standards and responsibility. Why were sub-prime loans granted to risky borrowers (many based on fraudulent loan applications) who subsequently defaulted?

Banks also need to continually reaffirm their standards in relation to how they manage their operations. It's quite clear that if the standards applied by banks fall, customer confidence is eroded.

In March 2006, economic factors led to an investigation into work-related stress at the Bank of New Zealand. Briefly, the resulting report explains how lack of staff and the constant pressure to meet unrealistic sales targets, by cross selling and selling to family and friends, were the main causes of staff stress. Setting sales targets or introducing 'pay for performance' may also compromise employees' compliance with stated banking standards.

There are three important tools that enable a bank to establish and maintain its standards: firstly, a code of conduct; secondly, clearly set out departmental operating procedures; and finally, a clearly communicated ethics policy.

A code of conduct provides all bank employees, from the executive team to the entry-level employees, with specific information about what is and is not acceptable business behaviour, with respect to receiving unsolicited gifts and benefits, waiver of fees, prior disclosure of possible conflicts of interest, and so on.

Departmental operating procedures provide the internal controls that ensure consistency and quality of bank performance by specifying step-by-step instructions on the procedures carried out by each department. For example, the operating procedures in a bank's loans department would specify the procedures to be followed by the bank loans officer in processing a loan.

Ethical behaviour is described by the International Dictionary of Banking and Finance (2000, p.137) as 'an action that conforms to the moral constraints of an industry or society … Professional ethics restrict a number of undesirable practices that are not strictly illegal.' An ethics policy should express the bank's underlying values. The World Bank Code of Professional Ethics, in a publication entitled Living Our Values (1999) 'is intended to serve as a guide for staff and managers to use in day-to-day interactions and decision making'. The focus of an ethics policy is relationships within and outside the bank.

This includes person-to-person relationships, workplace relationships, and the bank's relationship with the wider community. Many financial institutions have an ethics policy but few conduct 'ethics training', that is, training in dealing with unpredictable situations. Ethics education is not about teaching morality. It is about risk and risk management. It should also cover staff queries and matters arising from the code of conduct. The rules that inform banking practice are not static. The challenge for banks is to balance the business demands of profit-making with the need for good working relationships, both within the bank and with the wider community.

Now, I'm going to stop at this point. Does anybody have any questions?

Unit 11, Lesson 2, Exercise F 🎧 2.10

There is no doubt that fraud is a global concern. In 2005 Unisys conducted a survey into the increasing prevalence of online identity theft. At that time, 17% of US and 11% of UK consumers reported being a victim. In 2006 a Gartner Research survey found a 50% increase in ID theft victims compared to 2003. All the evidence shows that, as the acceptance of financial products such as credit cards grows, the risk of ID fraud also increases. What seems obvious is that banks (and their customers) have a responsibility for remaining vigilant and up to date with online security measures in order to protect themselves from Internet hackers.

Some people claim that biometric data, such as iris scans and fingerprints, could provide the answer. However, it could be argued that this will not solve the problem, as the usefulness of biometrics depends on the quality (and therefore the cost) of the machine and the technology used. Other people favour 'two-factor identification'. In addition to a password, confirmation by cellphone is required. Two-factor identification puts another step in the way of criminals.

Unit 11, Lesson 2, Exercise G 🎧 2.11

1 Good morning. Today I'm going to focus on banking standards. That is to say, I shall be looking at some of the factors which may affect, or compromise, the way banks operate in their day-to-day banking, including some of the fraudulent behaviour banks have to deal with.

2 Don't misunderstand me, I don't want to imply that banks, or their employees, commonly engage in fraudulent behaviour, but as we all know, banking scandals and crises are not uncommon.

3 It is fair to say that as a result of technological advancements banking operations are more complex.

4 Not only that, but globalization means banks need to be aware of the government policies of the country or countries with whom they operate.

5 So, in an attempt to keep this discussion of banking standards and responsibilities reasonably simple, I'm going to summarize a few of the more interesting problems banks may be exposed to.

6 Computer hacking has become widespread and increasingly more sophisticated to the extent that Internet fraud, through phishing, pharming, and spyware, is now a major area of concern for banks.

7 The process known as 'spear phishing' is a case in point.

8 For those of you unfamiliar with these terms, webopedia.com gives a good description.

9 Client education programmes can, to some degree, raise customers' awareness of new forms of fraud, and of the need to notify their bank, as soon as they receive suspect e-mails.

10 There is no doubt that fraud is a global concern.

11 Briefly, the resulting report explains how lack of staff and the constant pressure to meet unrealistic sales targets, by cross selling and selling to family and friends, were the main causes of staff stress.

12 A code of conduct provides all bank employees, from the executive team to the entry-level employees, with specific information about what is and is not acceptable business behaviour, with respect to receiving unsolicited gifts and benefits, waiver of fees, prior disclosure of possible conflicts of interest, and so on.

Unit 11, Lesson 3, Exercise A 2.12

bank se'curity

business oppor'tunities

computer 'hacking

data pro'tection

eco'nomic factors

'ethics policy

globali'zation factors

'unsolicited gifts

Unit 11, Lesson 3, Exercise B 2.13

Part 3

Turning now to the effect of economic factors on banking standards … Of course, a major concern is the development of new and changing financial instruments. This is partly a result of technological and globalization factors, and partly a result of deregulation of the banking industry. Deregulation means a reduction of government controls; therefore, we have to accept that banks must determine their own risk profile. But the question is: are banks capable of regulating themselves?

Some people claim that the current system has sufficient checks and balances. I'm afraid, however, that examples of lenders from around the world taking very little responsibility for their lending decisions suggest that this just isn't true. For example, those involved in the finance chain of the US sub-prime mortgages, from mortgage broker to investment bank, focused too much on the business opportunities. They didn't consider the consequences of mortgagees defaulting on their loans.

There are other examples from different parts of the world. On December 9, 2003, the Jakarta Post published a report on fraud, involving US$200 million, in export loans to a number of local companies by the state-owned BNI, Indonesia's second largest bank. The bank had failed to conduct proper credit appraisals before providing export loans to several local businessmen who used, as collateral, letters of credit guaranteed by banks in foreign countries, including Kenya. They claimed to be exporting commodities to Africa but I'm afraid that just wasn't true.

In another example, an article in The Economist, June 30, 2007, on the causes of the Asian Financial crisis of 1997, identified feeble regulation and supervision, alarming mismatches between assets and liabilities, wasteful investment, inadequate bank regulation, and corruption as contributing factors.

An audit by PricewaterhouseCoopers into Bank Bali at the time, uncovered 'numerous' indications of fraud. Key government officials (including the finance minister, and the central bank governor) were implicated. Bribery, in the form of unsolicited gifts and kickbacks to senior bank officials who approved loans, was commonplace at the time.

It's quite clear that all financial institutions, and banks in particular, need robust financial controls – especially when a significant amount of business activity is located in another jurisdiction. Some of the responsibility, for example, for the fraudulent use of Barings Bank's money by rogue trader, Nick Leeson, lies in the fact that the bank's London-based executives did not have controls in place to monitor the activities in their Singapore office. If banks don't take responsibility for what is happening and do something about it, governments will step in. The evidence for this lies in the fact that the Sarbanes-Oxley Act was rushed into US law in 2002, after the large bankruptcies of Enron (in which nine US banks were implicated) and WorldCom.

Unless they want to be subject to tighter government regulation, banks need to develop initiatives which appeal to their consumers' need for security, yet don't compromise the banks' profit-making objective. It is argued that banks have a moral responsibility to ensure that their clients' personal details and financial affairs are secure and that active controls are in place to provide total data protection from, for example, computer hacking. Continual advances in technology, particularly computer technology, mean this is an ongoing concern. Banks need to invest in highly skilled personnel whose job is to keep themselves up to date with the latest technology and threats to bank security. Many of these bank IT employees are relatively young technical people, yet the nature of their work will provide them with access to the personal and financial data of bank clients. It is therefore important that a comprehensive ethics policy and high banking standards are in place to guide these employees in the disclosure of this client data.

Now, I'm going to set you a task which will involve investigating some of the points I've raised. I want you to do some research into one of the following three topics which affect banking standards, namely, inadequate regulation and supervision; fraud and security problems; and deregulation. For your chosen topic, I would like you to identify causes and consequences. Secondly, I'd like you to suggest some solutions – in other words, what banking needs to think about to improve its standards. So, to repeat, your task is to identify the causes and consequences, and to suggest solutions.

Unit 11, Lesson 3, Exercise E 🎧 2.14

But the question is: are banks capable of regulating themselves? Some people claim that the current system has sufficient checks and balances. I'm afraid, however, that examples of lenders from around the world taking very little responsibility for their lending decisions suggest that this just isn't true.

It's quite clear that all financial institutions, and banks in particular, need robust financial controls. The evidence lies in the fact that the Sarbanes-Oxley Act was rushed into US law in 2002, after the large bankruptcies of Enron (in which nine US banks were implicated) and WorldCom.

Unit 11, Lesson 4, Exercise E 🎧 2.15

Extract 1

The lecturer we listened to last week introduced a number of interesting issues. In my part of the seminar, I would like to build on what he said about the impact of new technologies and talk specifically about cheque fraud. The advent of personal computers and PC-driven laser printers that can replicate documents with high resolutions has contributed significantly to a rise in cheque fraud. It's obvious that there's a lot the bank can do to prevent cheque fraud. For example, they should have a very clear policy on the duration and placement of stop payments. Performing cheque account reconciliations quickly may lead to early detection of fraudulent or questionable items. The reconciliation policies must include information on how to handle duplicate serial numbers, and on checking for numbers that are too short, too long, or in an unusual range, colour or size. The policy needs to clearly specify the notification process, if a suspect item is found, and the time in which it is to be dealt with. Time may be critical in achieving a satisfactory outcome. For the banks, the benefits of continuously updating the training of their cheque reconciliation staff, as well as having sufficient trained staff to deal with the volume of cheque fraud, will far outweigh the costs.

Extract 2

That seems like a very good point Majed is making. What I'd like to discuss is one important initiative for dealing with the opening of new accounts and the monitoring of existing ones. To hopefully avoid fraud losses and prevent money laundering, and to counter terrorism financing, bank staff should receive training in 'know your customer' (KYC) procedures.

A key aspect of KYC controls is monitoring a customer's transactions against their recorded profile and the history of their accounts. For this task, banks increasingly use specialized transaction monitoring software, particularly names-analysis software and trend-monitoring software. If unusual activity is identified, then due diligence processes, using all sources of information on the subject, including the Internet, are utilized to determine whether a transaction or activity is suspicious and should be reported to the authorities. Does anybody have any opinions or anything they would like to add?

Extract 3

Right. Thank you, Evie. I'm going to expand the topic by mentioning ethics and integrity. Because bank employees are exposed to significant sums of money, some are tempted into fraudulent behaviour. The research indicates, however, that it is the perceived examples from the bank's chief executives - that is, overt or covert messages regarding their work standards and ethics - that have the most influence on bank staff behaviour. Clearly then, the ethics policy must be communicated from the top of the organization downwards. Managers and departmental heads responsible for implementing the policies could attend ethical leadership courses. However, sometimes the message may be confusing. Let me try and make this clearer with an example. For instance, in February 2007 the Wall Street Journal reported that Bank of America was offering credit cards to illegal immigrants. While the bank argued that it was doing nothing illegal, critics said that they should not be helping people who violated the country's immigration laws, and that the bank was only concerned about getting the business of an untapped market of 10 to 20 million illegal immigrants. The question is: while the bank may have acted within the law, are its actions ethical? So to sum up, I would like to point out that it takes years to build a reputation and minutes to ruin it. Ethics is not a luxury but a necessity.

Extract 4

Well, I'm going to explain about detecting elder financial abuse, in the context of banking. I feel that this needs addressing as the population ages. Basically, it's financial abuse committed against people 65 years old and over. In the US, states have passed legislation requiring bank employees to report suspected cases of elder financial abuse. Some of the features of this phenomenon include: sudden changes in an elder person's bank accounts, or practices; uncharacteristic or unexplained withdrawals of large sums of money by an elder or someone representing them; large credit card transactions or cheques written to unusual recipients. Other examples may include large transfers of funds to a family member or acquaintance without reasonable explanation, new signatories to an elder person's account, or newly formed joint accounts with another person. Staff should also look for elderly people who appear nervous when accompanied by another person, or appear to be bullied, or give incoherent explanations for a withdrawal. Elderly people who appear confused about increases in credit card transactions, or about bank fees that have been incurred are possibly victims. Suspicion should be raised about signatures that look to be forged on financial transactions and applications for new items, for example, credit cards. It is in the bank's interest to take a proactive role by training their employees to recognize and report this. It also gives a positive message to the growing number of elderly customers. In my view, banks have a capacity to provide services to the community while making a legitimate profit.